SCIENTIFIC AMERICAN EXPLORES BIG IDEAS

COVID's Lasting Impacts

The Editors of *Scientific American*

SCIENTIFIC AMERICAN | EDUCATIONAL PUBLISHING

New York

Published in 2025 by Scientific American Educational Publishing
in association with **The Rosen Publishing Group**
2544 Clinton Street, Buffalo NY 14224

Contains material from Scientific American®, a division of Springer Nature America, Inc., reprinted by permission, as well as original material from The Rosen Publishing Group®.

First Edition

Scientific American
Lisa Pallatroni: Project Editor

Rosen Publishing
Danielle Haynes: Compiling Editor
Michael Moy: Senior Graphic Designer

Cataloging-in-Publication Data

Names: Scientific American, Inc.
Title: COVID's lasting impacts / edited by the Scientific American Editors.
Description: First edition. | New York : Scientific American Educational Publishing, 2025. | Series: Scientific American explores big ideas | Includes glossary and index.
Identifiers: ISBN 9781538312834 (pbk.) | ISBN 9781538312841 (library bound)| ISBN 9781538312858 (ebook)
Subjects: LCSH: COVID-19 (Disease)–Juvenile literature. | COVID-19 Pandemic, 2020–Juvenile literature. | COVID-19 (Disease)–Social aspects–Juvenile literature.
Classification: LCC RA644.C67 C685 2025 | DDC 614.5'92–dc23

Manufactured in the United States of America
Websites listed were live at the time of publication.

Cover: Lightspring/Shutterstock.com

CPSIA Compliance Information: Batch # CW25SA.
For Further Information contact Rosen Publishing at 1-800-237-9932.

CONTENTS

INTRODUCTION

For some people, it's a little hard to remember a time before the COVID-19 pandemic, which sent most of the world into a months-long lockdown and killed in excess of 7 million people. Starting at the beginning of 2020, everything was viewed through the lens of the virus: health, the government, scientific research, the environment, and even child care.

The articles in this book delve deeper into the lasting legacy of COVID-19 and how the world is dealing with the fallout. Many thousands of people are still experiencing the debilitating effects of the virus. Section 1, "Long COVID," explores some of these long-lasting effects of the disease, including brain fog, and how some doctors believe rates may be on the decline thanks to vaccines. Section 2, "The COVID Cycle," includes articles on how some people seem to be prone to repeated bouts of the virus, while others have remained largely unscathed. One article addresses a phenomenon known as Paxlovid rebound, in which those being treated with antiviral therapies sometimes end up getting sicker later as the disease progresses.

For some, the legacy of COVID lies in the scientific advancements made in doctors' efforts to find, treat, and prevent the spread of the virus. In Section 3, "Scientific Breakthroughs," articles look at how scientists came together to create new vaccines to treat unusual symptoms. Lockdowns also inspired creative solutions. Section 4, "Lockdown Legacy," looks at how the world attempted to keep going during the limitations caused by the virus. Telehealth and Zoom meetings became the new norm, and there was even a baby boom in some U.S. states.

Finally, Section 5 explores ideas for how governments and nongovernmental organizations can implement public health policies to prevent some of the difficulties that arose during the pandemic. Such policies could better limit the spread of future outbreaks and avoid devastating lockdowns.

Section 1: Long COVID

Longest-Ever COVID Infection Lasted More Than 600 Days

By Riis Williams

When the Omicron strain of SARS-CoV-2, the virus that causes COVID, was surging around the world in February 2022, a man infected with the variant was admitted to Amsterdam University Medical Center. He was 72 years old and had myelodysplastic and myeloproliferative overlap syndrome—a combination of disorders that disrupt proper blood cell production—and lymphoma. In the following 612 days, during which time he was in and out of the hospital, the man continued to test positive for COVID. His case is the longest consecutive COVID infection ever documented, according to a recent report by researchers at the University of Amsterdam.

The report details the evolution of the man's symptoms and his treatment course and how the Omicron variant developed more than 50 new mutations during the more than 20 months that the individual was infected. The report, which has not yet been published in a scientific journal, was presented this past weekend at the European Society of Clinical Microbiology and Infectious Diseases Global Congress in Barcelona.

"Chronic infections and viral evolution [are] commonly described in [the] literature, and there are other cases of immunocompromised patients who have had [COVID] infections for hundreds of days," says Magda Vergouwe, an M.D./Ph.D. candidate at the university's Center for Experimental and Molecular Medicine and lead author of the report. "But this is unique due to the extreme length of the infection ... and with the virus staying in his body for so long, it was possible for mutations to just develop and develop and develop."

The man, who unfortunately later died from complications of his underlying conditions—not COVID specifically—was first admitted to the hospital when he began experiencing COVID respiratory symptoms, including a cough, shortness of breath, and dangerously low blood oxygen levels. He had previously received three shots of the Moderna mRNA COVID vaccine, but his body contained no detectable antibodies. This is likely because of the immune-system-suppressing medications that he was taking to treat his lymphoma and blood condition, Vergouwe says. One of the drugs that he was taking, rituximab, targets abnormal cancer-causing B cells, but in the process it can also destroy their healthy counterparts, which are responsible for creating antibodies against infections.

Doctors prescribed the man multiple COVID treatment regimens, including sotrovimab, a monoclonal antibody that is approved by the European Medicines Agency. He had no measurable clinical response to any of the treatments and could not safely stop any of his other medications that might have been disrupting their effectiveness.

After about a month, however, the man's initial COVID symptoms waned on their own, and he was discharged to a rehabilitation center and eventually his own home to isolate. But he continued to test positive for COVID throughout those 20 months and at times developed new infections—such as bacterial pneumonia—that were likely complicated by COVID and required additional hospital stays. "It's important to note that in the end he did not die from his COVID-19," Vergouwe says. "But he did keep it with him for a very long period of time until then, and this is why we made sure to sample [the virus in his body] as much as we could."

The researchers analyzed 27 nasal swab samples taken from February 2022 through September 2023 and detected more than 50 new mutations to the original Omicron strain that infected the man. Vergouwe says that while that number can sound shocking, mutations to the SARS-CoV-2 genome are expected to evolve more quickly in those who are immunocompromised (the average mutation rate of the virus is estimated to be two mutations per person per month). What does make these mutations unusual, she notes, is how their features differed vastly from mutations observed in other people with COVID. She hypothesizes that the exceptional length of the individual's infection and his preexisting conditions allowed the virus to evolve extensively and uniquely.

But it's unlikely that the 50 new COVID mutations that emerged in this case will spread worldwide, says David Wohl, a professor of medicine in the division of infectious diseases at the University of North Carolina at Chapel Hill, who was not involved in the research. Viral mutation is common; a virus replicating in the human body rarely does so perfectly, and these slightly different versions are deemed mutants. Sometimes the changes to the virus are unhelpful for its survival and aren't perpetuated. Other times a mutant's new characteristic is beneficial to the virus and can help it overcome an infected person's immune response. The mutant becomes a greater threat and can turn into a variant of concern if it can hop from host to host, picking up new traits and defenses against antibodies.

In this case, the viral mutants did not have characteristics that increased its transmission, and there is no documentation that they infected any other people. In order for mutations to successfully spread and become as treacherous as the Omicron and Delta COVID variants, there needs to be a "perfect storm of bad things happening," Wohl says.

Lengthy COVID infections in immunocompromised people aren't particularly rare, Vergouwe says, and experts are continuing to survey these cases to track the development of mutations and better understand people's immune responses.

The best ways people at all risk levels for severe COVID can protect themselves remain staying up-to-date on vaccines and wearing high-quality masks in crowded areas. "New variants can potentially emerge from immunocompromised folks," Wohl says. "But variants also pop up from others [who are] not immunocompromised as [they] pass the virus to one another. This is part of the nature of the pandemic and how viruses just naturally exist and, unfortunately, evolve."

About the Author

Riis Williams is a New York City–based science journalist who specializes in climate, health and wildlife reporting. She formerly served as Scientific American's *news intern.*

Vaccination Dramatically Lowers Long COVID Risk

By Shannon Hall

At least 200 million people worldwide have struggled with long COVID: a slew of symptoms that can persist for months or even years after an infection with SARS-CoV-2, the virus that causes COVID. But research suggests that that number would likely be much higher if not for vaccines.

A growing consensus is emerging that receiving multiple doses of the COVID vaccine before an initial infection can dramatically reduce the risk of long-term symptoms. Although the studies disagree on the exact amount of protection, they show a clear trend: the more shots in your arm before your first bout with COVID, the less likely you are to get long COVID. One meta-analysis of 24 studies published in October, for example, found that people who'd had three doses of the COVID vaccine were 68.7 percent less likely to develop long COVID compared with those who were unvaccinated. "This is really impressive," says Alexandre Marra, a medical researcher at the Albert Einstein Israelite Hospital in Brazil and the lead author of the study. "Booster doses make a difference in long COVID."

It is also a welcome departure from earlier studies, which suggested that vaccines provided only a modest defense against long COVID. In 2022 Marra's team published a meta-analysis of six studies that found that a single dose of the COVID vaccine reduced the likelihood of long COVID by 30 percent. Now, that protection appears to be much greater.

A study published in November in the *BMJ* found that a single COVID vaccine dose reduced the risk of long COVID by 21 percent, two doses reduced it by 59 percent and three or more doses reduced it by 73 percent. Vaccine effectiveness clearly climbed with each successive dose. "I was surprised that we saw such a clear dose response," says Fredrik Nyberg, an epidemiologist at the

University of Gothenburg in Sweden and one of the co-authors of the study. "The more doses you had in your body before your first infection, the better." That lines up with the findings of several new studies, which similarly show this ladderlike benefit. Marra's October 2023 meta-analysis found that two doses reduced long COVID likelihood by 36.9 percent and three doses reduced it by 68.7 percent. And in a study published last year in the *Journal of the American Medical Association*, other researchers found that the prevalence of long COVID in health-care workers dropped from 41.8 percent in unvaccinated participants to 30 percent in those with a single dose, 17.4 percent with two doses, and 16 percent with three doses.

These studies were conducted in various countries with differing health-care systems, demographics, COVID vaccination uptake, and COVID prevalence. As such, Marra notes that the COVID vaccines' effectiveness against long COVID will vary and may not be generalizable to other settings. Still, the consistency of the studies' findings is telling—regardless of their settings, many studies agree that boosters provide potent protection against long COVID. Marra's recent meta-analysis, for example, showed that the prevalence of long COVID in the early years of the pandemic was consistently above 20 percent. Today rates of long COVID have dropped, likely thanks to increased immunity, milder variants, and improved treatment. Yet there is still a sharp divide between unvaccinated and vaccinated people. The prevalence of long COVID is currently 11 percent among those who are unvaccinated and 5 percent among those who have had two or more doses of the vaccine. "It is a significant difference for those who are unwilling to take the risk," he says.

The question is why. It could be that these vaccines help prevent severe COVID itself, which is a risk factor for long COVID. But that does not appear to be the whole story—in part because the boosters have also been shown to shield people who had only a mild COVID infection. Unfortunately, the precise mechanisms at play are hard to disentangle because the cause of long COVID itself is still cloaked in mystery. One possibility is that the virus lingers in the body, hiding in various organs—such as the gut or brain—and causing chronic inflammation. Another is that long COVID is an autoimmune disease in which the immune response triggered by the initial infection wages an extended war against the body, causing symptoms long after the initial infection has been cleared.

For both scenarios, boosters give people the upper hand, argues Akiko Iwasaki, an immunologist at Yale University who is co-leading a clinical trial on long COVID. That is because boosters enhance antibodies—increasing both their numbers and their ability to bind to the virus—as well as T and B immune cells that help fight the virus. With both components, "people who take the booster shots have an improved ability to fight off infection," Iwasaki says. And that is key, allowing the booster to quash a growing infection before it spirals out of control. "The more you can prevent the replication and spread of the virus within the body, the less chance the virus has to seed a niche—to establish reservoirs or cause excessive inflammation that leads to autoimmunity," she says.

Although it will take time to pinpoint the exact reason behind vaccines' protective effect against long COVID, many medical experts are hopeful that the new studies will help counter the spread of misinformation and disinformation about the COVID immunizations that has contributed to vaccine hesitancy. But experts also note that while vaccines reduce the risk of long COVID, they do not eradicate it, and protection may wane over time. "Breakthrough infections can still occur, and the dynamic of the virus—including the emergence of new variants—add complexity to the situation," Marra says. As such, he notes that it's important to continue to follow public health guidelines to minimize the impact of COVID, including the risk of long-term symptoms.

About the Author

Shannon Hall is an award-winning freelance science journalist based in the Rocky Mountains. She specializes in writing about astronomy, geology, and the environment.

The Brain Fog of Long COVID Is a Serious Medical Issue That Needs More Attention

By Emily Mendenhall & Kenton Kaplan

This isn't a fog. This is life under an ice sheet. The term *brain fog* has everyone I meet expecting I'll be better any day now."

This is what one of us (Ken) wrote in his journal about the periodic memory loss and inability to concentrate that he experienced throughout 2022, when he struggled with symptoms of long COVID.

Long COVID is a neurological disease that happens after people are no longer infected with SARS-CoV-2. Its prevalence appears to be between 15 percent and 30 percent, according to numerous studies. About 46 percent of people who have it report some type of memory disruption. People associate the term "brain fog" with confusion, trouble concentrating, anxiety, forgetting, and sometimes headaches. But the term has become a societal and medical catch-all for the vast and varied neurological, psychological, and emotional aspects of long COVID. When someone feels hazy, tired, and distracted, it's called brain fog. Yet, when the fatigue remains and memory goes every 10 minutes, it's also called brain fog. By calling all long COVID-related cognitive or psychological dysfunctions brain fog, it diminishes what people like Ken have experienced.

When the other of us (Emily) was sick, she would forget the occasional word or lose her focus, which are common in mild cases of long COVID. This lasted around a month. But for Ken, long COVID was more than a year of inconsistent but extreme memory loss, extreme fatigue, and immunosuppression that led to several emergency department visits. Under the current understanding, we both had brain fog, even though our symptoms were radically different.

This idea that brain fog is "fuzziness" and not serious predates the pandemic and makes it harder for people who need short and long-term disability accommodations to get them. This was Ken's experience, as two professors did not believe he had long COVID or needed accommodations to finish the academic year. All brain fog is not the same, and it's time society creates different ways of explaining how people experience the cognitive symptoms of long COVID so that those with severe symptoms are taken more seriously and receive the physical, financial, and workplace or academic support they need to recover.

As a medical anthropologist, Emily was interested in learning more about how people experience long COVID symptoms to disentangle them from how society perceives the condition. Ken's experience was at the center of this project; he journaled for more than a year about his symptoms, including what we believe was severe brain fog. Ken interviewed 22 people living with long COVID to better understand how their experiences aligned with or diverged from his own.

We found people described brain fog differently from the mild forgetfulness that has become the popular definition.

A 44-year-old father described to Ken how becoming completely debilitated by long COVID transformed his everyday life. He said, "When I'm having a brain fog day, I have to ask my wife to bring me a stockpile of daily necessities in bed before she leaves for work. I can't stand up, I can't move, and I can't function for hours, even days sometimes." He described headaches and pain at five months after his initial infection and said that he felt worse having long COVID than COVID itself. Nineteen of the 22 people we interviewed struggled to complete routine tasks at some point during their illness.

Ken struggled for four months with coursework at Georgetown University as he only remembered things in 10-minute intervals. Fifteen people we spoke to described experiencing similar memory loss. They also described chronic nerve pain, severe headaches, and episodes of dizziness, nausea, and fainting. This is alarming, because new research has shown that long COVID can result in neurological damage and neurocognitive dysfunction that may cause lifelong impairment.

Despite the specter of lifelong impairment, many of the people we interviewed said that people rarely took their symptoms seriously.

A 67-year-old woman with a history of epilepsy told Ken: "I feel like I'm living entire days and weeks of my life in that postictal epileptic haze. I'm drowsy and confused, usually with splitting migraines. But I've had to start telling people I'm having epileptic episodes when I'm struggling with brain fog because they believe epilepsy is real. Telling the truth and saying I'm dealing with brain fog is more work than it's worth."

We need to understand the different types of brain fog to help classify them for practical purposes, but also to legitimize these cognitive differences for the sake of accommodating people with long COVID. This is not easy to do because there is so much variability in this disease; the virus affects multiple parts of the body, and researchers and clinicians have identified hundreds of symptoms. Creating different classes of brain fog, then, requires us to lump together symptoms that could be severe, for example, but still variable from person to person.

Long COVID is a federally recognized disability. Yet, 16 of the 17 people who reported brain fog in our study described feeling disbelieved. Nine of the 13 people we interviewed who sought disability accommodations faced significant barriers to access. At Georgetown, Brittney Klein, who manages disability accommodations and worked with Ken to help him get through the spring and fall semesters in 2022, told us that the school's academic resource center has had a number of long COVID accommodation requests. Ken is not an outlier, by any stretch.

In this project we found a gulf between clinicians' perceptions of the severity of brain fog and the perceptions of the people who have it. So many people feel alone and dismissed–this is reinforced on message boards, blog posts, and Twitter feeds. Categorization of the most severe symptoms is a way not only to legitimize people's neurocognitive dysfunction but also to elevate their need for intervention. We plan to publish a more extensive analysis of our findings in a medical journal.

We still don't know much about brain fog, and there are major gaps in how we think about long COVID. However, we know for certain that brain fog is real. And brain fog is multiple things.

More than one year after his long COVID diagnosis, Ken still experiences sporadic memory loss and difficulty processing information. He has come to accept his struggles with brain fog as a continuing part of daily life, even as his physical health has mostly returned to normal. He now wishes he had taken medical leave during the worst of his long COVID. Regardless, identifying the complexity and diversity of symptoms people manage with brain fog, and creating a better nomenclature around that diversity would provide a clearer path for legitimizing medical leave and accommodations, and in the end, hopefully, help people lead productive lives as they manage this new normal.

This is an opinion and analysis article, and the views expressed by the author or authors are not necessarily those of Scientific American.

About the Authors

Emily Mendenhall is a medical anthropologist and professor at the Edmund A. Walsh School of Foreign Service at Georgetown University. She was recently awarded a Guggenheim Fellowship for Anthropology and Cultural Studies for her work on COVID.

Kenton Kaplan is a senior in the Edmund A. Walsh School of Foreign Service at Georgetown University.

Blood Clotting Proteins Might Help Predict Long COVID Brain Fog

By Sara Reardon

Many people who have long COVID—a condition in which health issues persist months after infection—report struggling with "brain fog," recurring memory and concentration lapses that make it difficult to function in everyday life. Now a new study has found these cognitive problems could result from blood clots triggered by infection, possibly through mechanisms like those that cause some types of dementia. These clots leave telltale protein signatures in blood, suggesting that testing for them could help predict, diagnose, and possibly even treat long COVID.

The findings, published on Thursday in *Nature Medicine*, suggest that existing blood tests for detecting these proteins could help physicians recognize long COVID (although some experts caution that long COVID's symptoms and causes likely vary among individuals). Up to 15 percent of people who contract SARS-CoV-2, the virus that causes COVID, go on to develop long COVID symptoms that can last for months or years. The condition has proved difficult to treat—or even diagnose—because of the mishmash of reported symptoms such as brain fog, fatigue, respiratory problems, and numerous other effects. It's still unclear whether the virus sticks around in the body or the initial infection triggers another reaction, such as an autoimmune response, that leads to the continuing symptoms.

To look into this question, lead study author and psychiatrist Maxime Taquet of the University of Oxford followed more than 1,800 people in the U.K. who were hospitalized for COVID between 2020 and 2021. Taquet and his colleagues checked in with the patients six and 12 months after their initial infection to monitor any prolonged symptoms and give them a cognitive test designed to diagnose disorders such as Alzheimer's.

When the researchers examined blood tests taken while the patients were hospitalized, they found that blood from people who still had brain fog six or 12 months after infection tended to have elevated levels of at least one of two proteins in their blood. The first protein, called D-dimer, is produced when blood clots break down in the body. Although patients with high levels of D-dimer reported memory problems, they did not score lower on cognitive tests. They were more likely to have shortness of breath and fatigue than other patients, however. Taquet suspects these effects could have been caused by blood clots in the lungs, which can also lead to low oxygen levels in the brain.

The second protein, fibrinogen, is produced in the liver and causes clotting to stop bleeding. Patients who had elevated fibrinogen levels during active COVID infection not only reported memory impairment but also scored poorly on the cognitive test. On average, people in this group scored under 86.7 percent six months after infection—a test result that could indicate dementia. Taquet says these findings suggest that either fibrinogen caused blood clots in the brain or that clots elsewhere in the body affected the brain, causing more severe cognitive symptoms.

Blood tests for both D-dimer and fibrinogen are already standard around the world, so researchers had plenty of available data to check whether the same phenomenon occurred in other groups of patients. In a separate analysis, the team examined health records from nearly 50,000 people in the U.S.—including some who had taken blood tests for fibrinogen or D-dimer before the pandemic started. Brain fog with elevated levels of D-dimer, they found, only occurred in people who had had COVID. But elevated fibrinogen seemed to correlate with brain fog whether or not a person previously had COVID, which indicated that cognitive problems caused by other conditions may also involve fibrinogen.

The new findings are "very exciting," says Resia Pretorius, a physiologist at Stellenbosch University in South Africa. Her own research has found links between brain fog in long COVID and "microclots" in the blood. These clots often contain misfolded fibrinogen proteins that prevent the clots from breaking down, and this effect can clog blood vessels and block oxygen flow to the brain and other organs. Pretorius suspects that SARS-CoV-2's infamous spike protein interacts with the fibrinogen protein and causes it to change its shape.

Fibrinogen has previously been linked to cognitive difficulties, particularly vascular dementia. Studies have also shown that mice injected with fibrinogen can develop cognitive problems. It's unclear whether dissolving clots could reverse existing damage to the brain or whether the lack of oxygen kills neurons permanently, says Sidney Strickland, an Alzheimer's researcher at Rockefeller University in New York City.

Strickland says it's possible that clot-dissolving anticoagulant medications (often called blood thinners) could help alleviate long COVID symptoms, yet this has not been directly tested in clinical trials. He adds that these drugs need to be used cautiously because they can increase the risk of fatal blood loss. "You definitely want blood clots when you need them," Strickland says, "but not after the fact."

Blood thinners are a blunt instrument that affects several different ways in which the body can clot blood. Strickland's lab is developing antibodies that target just one of these pathways: the one that involves fibrinogen. These treatments shouldn't cause hemorrhages like generalized anticoagulants do, he says. Such treatments could be tested in those with long COVID, he adds, but his lab is still gearing up for clinical trials in people with dementia.

In the meantime, Strickland says, researchers still don't know what the exact relationship between COVID and fibrinogen is or what the protein does during long COVID. It may cause lung problems that affect blood flow or leaks in the blood-brain barrier. "We need to have a lot more information," Strickland says.

Avindra Nath, a neuroimmunologist at the National Institute of Neurological Disorders and Stroke, says the new results are interesting. He is skeptical about the blood clotting proteins' role in long COVID, however. Nath notes that the study only included people whose COVID infection was so severe that they were hospitalized and likely had organ damage. Long COVID can also occur in people who experienced few symptoms during active infection, he says, and their long-term conditions may have different causes. Nath's group has found blood clots in the brains of people who died of COVID, but he says more research is needed to determine if these clots caused their symptoms.

In the meantime, some physicians have noticed that blood-thinning medications may help certain long COVID patients. David Joffe, a respiratory physician at Royal North Shore Hospital in Sydney, Australia, says he prescribes anticoagulants because they tend to work better at restoring brain function in some long COVID patients than other treatments–although he also says that they need to be used carefully because of their inherent risks.

Joffe adds that the condition is difficult to study and treat because its symptoms vary so much. "Long COVID is lots of things," he says. "As a physician, I don't see two patients who are identical."

The variety of symptoms could be caused by different systems that the virus triggers, Joffe says. COVID infection has been linked to metabolic problems caused by cell damage and inflammation in the brain, as well as autoimmune conditions in which the immune system attacks the body. But the virus can also *suppress* the immune system, allowing underlying conditions to become active and cause their own array of symptoms.

Long COVID "is so much more complicated than people imagine," Joffe says.

Taquet says his team's results don't prove blood clots and vascular problems are the root of long COVID. "There is room for other hypotheses as well," he says. His group is now working with brain-imaging data from people with long COVID that could reveal more precisely where blood clots occur, as well as a more sensitive cognitive test that could show how brain impairment happens over time.

About the Author

Sara Reardon is a freelance journalist based in Bozeman, Mont. She is a former staff reporter at Nature, New Scientist *and* Science *and has a master's degree in molecular biology.*

A Tsunami of Disability Is Coming as a Result of Long COVID

By Claire Pomeroy

Even as U.S. policy makers and business leaders seek to put the COVID pandemic in the rearview mirror with the help of highly effective vaccines, a fundamental policy and planning gap is looming. Many who survive the initial viral illness suffer debilitating long-term sequelae. Unlike the common cold or even influenza, this virus causes a bewildering array of symptoms that persist long after the acute illness is resolved and can render some affected unable to resume their usual activities. As scientists and clinicians continue to delineate the "long-haul" course of COVID, policy makers and planners must anticipate and prepare for the impact of this new cause of disability, including its implications for federal and private worker's compensation and disability insurance programs and support services.

Consider the numbers we know. At least 34 million Americans (and probably many more) have already contracted COVID. An increasing number of studies find that greater than one-fourth of patients have developed some form of long COVID. (In one study from China, three-quarters of patients had at least one ongoing symptom six months after hospital discharge, and in another report more than half of infected health-care workers had symptoms seven to eight months later.) Initial indications suggest that the likelihood of developing persistent symptoms may not be related to the severity of the initial illness; it is even conceivable that infections that were initially asymptomatic could later cause persistent problems.

Common long-term symptoms include fatigue; respiratory problems; "brain fog"; cardiac, renal, and gastrointestinal issues; and loss of smell and taste. Surprising manifestations continue to emerge, such as the recent realization that infection may precipitate diabetes.

For some, symptoms have now continued for many months with no apparent end in sight, with many survivors fearing that they will simply have to adjust to a "new normal." More and more sufferers have not been able to return to work, even months after their initial illness. While the number of patients with persistent illness remains undetermined this early in the pandemic, estimates suggest that millions of Americans may enter the ranks of the permanently disabled.

The related health care and disability costs are also still unknowable. How many "long haulers" will never be able to return to work? How many will need short-term disability payments? How many will be permanently disabled and become dependent on disability programs? As increasing numbers of younger people become infected, will we see an entire generation of chronically ill? We must actively work to better understand the size and scope of the problem and begin planning now.

In addition to the personal suffering, long-term disability comes with a staggering price tag–including increased health-care costs; reduction or loss of employment; and economic strain on worker's compensation and disability support programs. It's been estimated that as much as 30 percent of the COVID health burden could arise from COVID-induced disability. As physician and University of Massachusetts medical professor Steven Martin recently told NPR, "If we end up with a million people with ongoing symptoms that are debilitating, that is a tremendous burden for each of these individuals, but also for our health-care system and our society."

Current U.S. disability programs appear ill-equipped to deal with this new stream of patients with chronic disability. Patients and employers alike can be overwhelmed by the inherent bureaucracy of the system, including worker's compensation, Social Security disability, and private disability insurance. For example, it is extremely difficult to pinpoint if workers contracted infection at their place of employment or in the community; limited access to testing means that many sufferers are unable to document their initial infection; and the Social Security Administration (SSA) requirements that the impairments must last or be expected to last at least 12 months and prevent "substantial, gainful" activity are daunting. But we cannot be short-sighted; barriers to disability support can exacerbate the severity of the medical problems and prolong the time in which patients are unable to return to their normal activities.

Here's what we need now:

- Research to better understand disability inflicted by long COVID. Scientists are partnering with patient groups such as Survivor Corps to better define these syndromes, and the NIH has called for proposals supported by the $1.15 billion in funding recently provided by Congress. We need to prioritize health economics studies to determine the financial implications of disability associated with the virus.
- Clinical services to manage long COVID. Clinics to care for "long haulers" are being opened but must be adequately staffed and funded. Both the CDC and AMA recently released guidelines for care. Coordinated collection of data on a national (and global) level will accelerate insights.
- Worker's compensation programs and private disability insurance. A national consensus on criteria for qualifying for payments is key. Insurance plan administrators should use health economics research to prepare for future costs.
- Federal disability programs. Analysis of the likely number of patients who will require short- and long-term disability payments and services should be at the front of the SSA's agenda, followed by modeling of the funding needed to support them. Requirements (including types of medical documentation and waiting periods) to quality for aid also need to be reexamined.

It's understandable that we don't yet have all the issues related to COVID-associated disability figured out; we haven't fully grasped all the implications of this pernicious (and still somewhat mysterious) malady. After all, since early 2020, we've been struggling to address the immediate crisis and how to deal with the new problems that arise day by day. But the time has come to proactively plan for what will certainly be the enormous new impact that long-haul COVID will have on our disability programs.

This is an opinion and analysis article; the views expressed by the author or authors are not necessarily those of Scientific American.

About the Author

Claire Pomeroy, M.D., M.B.A., is an infectious disease physician and researcher and president of the Lasker Foundation, which is dedicated to advancing medical research. During her academic career, her research focused on HIV/AIDS.

Long COVID Rates Appear to Be Decreasing

By Shannon Hall

Tens of millions of people in the U.S. have struggled with long COVID: a suite of symptoms that can persist long after an initial COVID infection and impact one's day-to-day life. Typically, these "long haulers" experience fatigue, difficulty concentrating, and joint pain. At its worst, however, the syndrome can leave them bedridden.

Now studies suggest the rates of long COVID may be dropping. Although the investigations were not designed to assess the reason for this trend, scientists suspect the downturn is a result of increased immunity to SARS-CoV-2 (the virus that causes COVID), milder variants of that pathogen and improved treatments. It is a welcome reprieve, but the decline does not help the millions of people who are already suffering from long COVID. Moreover, experts warn that the risk is still not zero. And without a clear explanation for the downward trend, it is unclear whether it will continue.

"You have to be vigilant," says Paul Elliott, an epidemiologist at Imperial College London's School of Public Health. "You can't just relax these days and be done."

There is reason for hope, however. Elliott and his team recently reported that people infected during the pandemic's Omicron wave were 88 percent less likely to develop long COVID, compared with those infected with the original strain that emerged in Wuhan, China. The research, published in October in *Nature Communications*, is the latest in a growing number of studies that point to a downswing in the debilitating condition. This summer, the U.S. Centers for Disease Control and Prevention noted that the proportion of people infected with SARS-CoV-2 who went on to develop long COVID dropped from 18.9 percent in June 2022 to 11 percent in January 2023. And just a few months before that, European researchers found that the risk of long COVID among cancer patients fell from

19.1 percent in 2020 to 6.2 percent in early 2022. Other studies show similar findings.

Although the studies disagree on absolute numbers, experts argue that the downhill trend is real—that the likelihood of any individual developing long COVID has fallen since the beginning of the pandemic. The question is why.

To start, greater population immunity—whether from infection, vaccination, or both—has likely provided protection against lingering symptoms. There is no question that vaccines have provided a strong defense against the virus over the past three years. And multiple studies suggest that vaccination also reduces the chances of developing long COVID—especially for those who stay up-to-date on their shots. The study on cancer patients, for example, found that the risk of developing long COVID was highest before vaccines against the disease were available and that participants who had received a booster were less likely to develop long COVID than those who were only partially vaccinated. Moreover, a study published just last week found that three or more doses of a COVID vaccine reduced the risk of long COVID by 73 percent, compared with 21 percent after just one dose. And while research is inconclusive on whether repeat infections confer protection, a single infection mixed with vaccination—otherwise known as hybrid immunity—likely reduces future infections and disease.

"At the population level, we are developing immune responses to the virus," says Akiko Iwasaki, an immunologist at the Yale School of Medicine. "The baseline immunity is different from when the pandemic first started."

We are also dealing with different viral variants. Many scientists believe that the intrinsic features of the different SARS-CoV-2 strains make them more or less likely to cause long COVID. Thus, many long COVID studies broke their data down not by infection date but by the dominant variant at the time. And some suggested that the severity of long COVID was far worse for those infected at the very start of the pandemic. One investigation compared Swiss hospital workers in May 2022—roughly six months after the Omicron variant first appeared—with workers who had been infected with the original strain in 2020. It found that the latter had far more lingering symptoms than those who were infected more recently. "I really think there is something to this variant, to Omicron, that makes it less aggressive," says Philipp Kohler, an infectious disease specialist at St. Gallen Cantonal Hospital in Switzerland and co-senior author of the study.

In some ways, the findings are not a surprise. During acute illness, Omicron is much less likely than earlier strains to land patients in the hospital with severe symptoms, which researchers know is a major risk factor for long COVID. Mild cases can also lead to long COVID, however, causing scientists to argue that another factor is at play. One hypothesis suggested in animal studies is that Omicron targets cells in the upper respiratory tract—causing coldlike symptoms in the nose and throat—whereas earlier forms of the virus targeted the lower respiratory tract and even involved other organs, where they continued to replicate and cause long-term symptoms.

Finally, treatments may have chipped away at long COVID incidence as well. Antivirals can now help to corral the virus early in an infection, thus reducing both its acute severity and its long-term impacts. In March 2023 a study involving more than 280,000 veterans with COVID found that those who were given the drug Paxlovid in the first five days of symptoms had an about 25 percent lower risk of developing long COVID than a control group. And a more recent study found that people who were overweight who received another drug called metformin, which also has antiviral properties, were 41 percent less likely to develop long COVID than those who received a placebo. Yale Medicine cardiologist Erica Spatz, who was not involved in the metformin study, was so impressed by the results that she now prescribes it to any COVID patients concerned about long COVID.

Yet for the most part, doctors are not widely ordering these drugs, meaning that they are probably not the main culprit behind the society-wide long COVID decline. And disentangling the two other hypotheses—population-level immunity and an intrinsic change to the virus—will be a challenge. Ziyad Al-Aly, a clinical epidemiologist at Washington University in St. Louis, who has led several studies of long COVID and was senior author of the metformin paper, would like to see an investigation that would cover the entire pandemic—one that enrolls patients who suffered long COVID following infections with every variant and thoroughly documents their vaccination, infection, and antiviral history to tease out the actual reason behind this change. He notes that such a study would not be easy, particularly because COVID testing and tracking have recently slowed, so long COVID patients are likely being undercounted. (Many of the previously mentioned papers avoided this issue because they stopped collecting data before the slowdown in testing.) But Al-Aly argues that such a study is feasible. It is also crucial if we want to know whether the long COVID downswing will continue.

Many argue that if population immunity is key, then long COVID cases could continue to drop. That is assuming vaccination uptake does not deteriorate further, however. "We cannot have our cake and eat it, too," Al-Aly says. "We cannot say vaccinations reduce the risk of long COVID by some percent and then abandon them—as is looking very likely—and expect long COVID to continue to decline."

But if the variant is more important, the future of long COVID will be the result of evolutionary chance. The virus will continue to mutate, and the next variant could be far more severe than Omicron and thus drive long COVID rates—not to mention deaths and hospitalizations—up again. Yet even in this dire case, Iwasaki says there is promise. If you are vaccinated, she says, you might be able to withstand a more dangerous variant. "That is my hope," Iwasaki says. "Currently there is nothing to go against that hope. But we can't be too comfortable. We can't assume that the future variants will be very mild."

And even if we are lucky, many experts argue that a dwindling risk is still a very real one. Nicole Ford, a senior health scientist at the CDC, who led the agency's investigation of long COVID earlier this year, notes that at the end of the study period in June 2023, roughly one in 10 adults who previously reported a COVID infection were still suffering from persistent symptoms. Of those, one in four had difficulty performing day-to-day activities—an alarming find, given that treatment is still lacking, and some patients have yet to fully recover. "The take-home from this study is that long COVID is common," Ford says. "It can impact absolutely anyone."

About the Author

Shannon Hall is an award-winning freelance science journalist based in the Rocky Mountains. She specializes in writing about astronomy, geology, and the environment.

What Tony Fauci Says about Long COVID and Other Postviral Illnesses

By Emily Mendenhall

The first person I met with long COVID was Kenton Kaplan, a student I was mentoring at Georgetown University. Without much warning, he had called me in January 2022 to drop out of our departmental honors program. As we talked over the next year and a half, he told me about debilitating fatigue, dizziness, and intense memory inconsistencies. He and his doctors believed that these symptoms were related to a COVID infection he likely caught at a New Year's Eve party.

Kaplan recovered and graduated with honors from Georgetown, but since meeting him, I've encountered many other people with long COVID—a syndrome of neurological, psychological, and physical issues that lasts long after the disease-causing virus, SARS-CoV-2, is gone. As a medical anthropologist, I've been fascinated by this postviral illness as both a sociocultural and a biological phenomenon. Millions of people seem to have it, even as some health-care professionals still believe postviral syndromes are "all in your head." I believe that even I have had some form of it—for several months after my first COVID infection, I was struck with anxiety, depression, and fatigue that eventually passed. I have spent hundreds of hours thinking about long COVID and interviewing people—patients, caregivers, physicians, nurses, academics, and policymakers—about their firsthand experiences.

One of the physicians I interviewed was Anthony Fauci, former head of the National Institute of Allergy and Infectious Diseases (NIAID). He is currently a faculty member at Georgetown. As part of the book I am now writing on contested chronic illnesses, we talked about postviral illnesses such as long COVID and myalgic encephalomyelitis/chronic fatigue syndrome (ME/CFS) and the challenge of understanding our body after an infection has ravaged it. I was surprised to learn that postviral illnesses have been on the embattled doctor's radar for about 50 years and that early research on these illnesses fell by the wayside as we struggled to understand their causes.

Fauci and I met over Zoom. I was right on time, albeit a bit disheveled. He, however, was put together and already waiting for me, ready to talk about the question of whether postviral illnesses such as long COVID are real.

Fauci told me how, when he arrived at the National Institutes of Health in 1968, he would see patients who had interesting "symptomatology," as he called it: messed-up bodily systems from brain to gut, including the kidneys, heart, blood, and nerves. This, he thinks, was perhaps his first concentrated look at what we would initially call chronic fatigue syndrome and eventually refer to as ME/CFS. Half of the people who experience chronic fatigue for several months or years have also had one or more of the following diagnoses: infections, anemia, thyroid dysfunction, diabetes mellitus, or cancer. And neuroscientists think that symptoms such as fatigue likely reflect a combination of many factors triggered by one event (such as SARS-CoV-2 infection) in people with chronic stressors, traumas that irreversibly affect the body or previous infections that linger through viral reservoirs (infected cells that do not actively produce viral particles).

Fauci told me, "This was before chronic fatigue syndrome ... even had a name.... [People were very sick] following a variety of what they perceived as viral infections." He said that back then we didn't have the diagnostics that we do now and that "there would be things about their demeanor and their ability to function, which were markedly compromised for variable periods of time."

I found this off-the-cuff comment to be striking because it meant that ME/CFS activists have been struggling for at least *five decades* to get recognition for their disabilities despite having what medical anthropologist Emily Lim Rogers described in a 2022 paper as the "dual-pronged challenge" of people with ME/CFS confronting "stigma caused by its lack of biological verification and societal acceptance" and doing so "in bodies that are exhausted."

Fauci said, however, that he and other infectious disease physician-scientists were soon swooped up into the still-ongoing global emergency of HIV/AIDS, leaving relatively less time and resources to devote to chronic, debilitating but non-fatal conditions. These illnesses frequently don't get the attention they deserve and it leaves many people suffering without the possibility of a diagnosis, let alone a cure.

We talked about more recent COVID cohort studies showing that more women are affected by long COVID than men. "Perhaps they are more susceptible to the dysregulation of whatever immune response is triggering ... long COVID," Fauci told me.

These gendered trends should not be surprising. In addition to long COVID and ME/CFS, chronic Lyme disease, multiple sclerosis, and autoimmune diseases such as lupus affect women more often. For centuries women have been dismissed, ignored, and punished for thinking differently about our body than the dominant culture does. This is more intense for women whose race, class, gender, sexuality, nationality, documentation status, and so on differs from their doctor's. But this evidence simply can't be set aside.

Because long COVID is often described as a neurological disease, an idea that is intriguing to me is related to the vagal nerves. These are responsible for many of the automatic functions in our body, such as breathing, standing and calming ourselves. Mike VanElzakker, a neuroscientist at Harvard Medical School, has argued that perhaps SARS-CoV-2 tricks the immune response by linking to this nerve bundle, making the body think it's under attack when in fact it is relatively healthy. This would mean that the vagal nerves' calming action is delayed–so the panic, heart palpitations, and constant anxiety many people have described to me make sense. Certainly more research on women's nervous systems and the interplay of immunology, neurology, and anthropology is imperative.

A lingering question is whether long COVID and ME/CFS are the same thing. Fauci emphasized what makes long COVID distinct from ME/CFS, even when the symptoms are the same, is the presence of a specific virus and the knowledge of when the infection occurred. He told me that historically, we didn't have the ability to pinpoint what infectious agent had caused a person's ME/CFS. We could maybe see what antibodies a person had against different viruses, but we never knew exactly when the infectious event happened, so we couldn't say with any certainty what caused someone's disease.

Finally, Fauci emphasized to me how important it is to do more research on postviral syndromes and, specifically, on how long COVID affects people differently. He told me, "There is going to be a group of people that, somehow or another ... have a genetic predisposition, just the way you have a genetic predisposition to diabetes or to rheumatoid arthritis or to lupus.... When [these people] get a viral infection, [it] somehow dysregulates [multiple functions and organ systems]."

But the key, he said, would be the kind of long-range, multiple-year funding that isn't necessarily dependent on a result for renewal—the type of funding that has existed in the past where so long as the work was good, he said, the researcher's job would be safe. We talked about how current funding structures don't really support this kind of open-ended research.

I was struck throughout the interview by Fauci's candor. During the pandemic, seemingly every word he uttered was interpreted with a political edge. I almost laughed when he breezily said near the end, "I am just giving you my scientific opinion in my experience as an immunology, virology, infectious disease guy." Having served NIAID for *five decades*, advised seven presidents, led the nation through several pandemics and set a high bar for what a scientific leader can do, I think that with his words, we can now put to rest the question of whether long COVID is real.

This is an opinion and analysis article, and the views expressed by the author or authors are not necessarily those of Scientific American.

About the Author

Emily Mendenhall is a medical anthropologist and professor at the Edmund A. Walsh School of Foreign Service at Georgetown University. She was recently awarded a Guggenheim Fellowship for Anthropology and Cultural Studies for her work on COVID.

Section 2: The COVID Cycle

How Risky Are Repeat COVID Infections? What We Know So Far

By Meghan Bartels

The specter of COVID has haunted the globe for four years now—the disease has killed at least 7 million people worldwide. Yet the pandemic's long-term effects are still hazy—because when it comes to a novel virus such as SARS-CoV-2, which causes COVID, scientists still have a lot to learn.

What we do know is that COVID is here to stay—and that catching it doesn't give people permanent immunity. Four years into the pandemic, researchers and clinicians know that people are racking up multiple infections, but the long-term consequences of repeatedly getting the virus aren't yet clear. Fortunately, both individuals and governments have strategies to avoid some infections—if they use them.

"However you slice it, whatever long-term health effect you look at, the risk [from reinfection] is not zero," says Ziyad Al-Aly, a clinical epidemiologist at Washington University in St. Louis. "The truth is that, yes, we're sick and tired of the virus, we're sick and tired of the pandemic—but it's still here. It's still hurting people."

In the U.S. alone, more than 1.1 million people have died of COVID since the pandemic began, according to the Centers for Disease Control and Prevention. The agency is no longer tracking infections at the community level, but in mid-January it reported that nearly 4 percent of deaths nationwide were caused by COVID.

And while the winter wave of infections appears to be waning, the world missed its chance to make COVID disappear. "This ugly guest isn't going to leave us any time soon," Al-Aly says. "It's going to be here probably for decades."

Early on in the pandemic, scientists hoped that COVID would be the sort of disease for which vaccination or infection creates immunity that lasts for years or a lifetime. But the SARS-CoV-2 virus had other plans. Vaccination and, to a lesser degree, infection make you less vulnerable to catching the virus and having a severe case, but that protection wanes over time.

"One infection does protect you against future infections" but not completely, says Jamie Rylance, a physician on the World Health Organization's clinical management team. The SARS-CoV-2 virus mutates rapidly, so a person's immune system can't necessarily fully fight off a new infection, even if it's been primed by a recent bout with a different strain. The same holds true for vaccinations: although initial shots and boosters help a person's immune system respond more effectively to an infection and reduce the odds of a serious COVID case, current COVID vaccines can't prevent infection completely.

Complicating things further, COVID often triggers asymptomatic infections, which helped the virus continue to spread early in the pandemic even in places where governments established relatively strict containment protocols. And four years into the pandemic, many people are testing for COVID less often and tests miss many asymptomatic cases, making them even harder to identify. So, people have likely been infected more times than they know.

"We don't know how often we're getting reinfected because we have some protection from vaccination or even past infection," says Maria Van Kerkhove, interim director of the WHO's department of Epidemic and Pandemic Preparedness and Prevention. She doesn't think that's something to be complacent about, however. "We know that when the virus enters our body, it affects multiple organ systems," she says.

The combination of evidence on COVID and the long-term impacts of other viruses paints a grim picture of what it might mean to experience regular COVID infections.

"Every time you get infected [with COVID], it does harm to the body in some way," says Avindra Nath, a neurologist at the National Institutes of Health who has led research on long COVID and other postviral conditions. For example, a pulmonary infection can leave scars in the lungs or trigger blood clots. COVID may also interfere with the immune system itself, he says. Nath notes that the protective sheaths of many viruses include regions that can interfere with the immune system. Separately, one study that followed up with participants after a flu infection found that in about 30 percent of people, the immune system remained somewhat impaired two months later.

And because COVID is still relatively new, scientists realistically have no idea what happens 10, 20, or even 30 years after an infection, much less multiple bouts. "What we need to be able to track is the complications of pulmonary function [and] cardiac function five years from now, 10 years from now," Van Kerkhove says.

Frustratingly, we may never have a clear sense of the damage COVID reinfections are causing, says Sunil Ahuja, an infectious disease specialist at University of Texas Health Science Center at San Antonio. "To ascribe cause and effect is very challenging," he says of potential long-term consequences of repeated bouts with COVID. During the span of time between infections, "they've also had many other things happen to them, too."

Some viruses can hide out in the body and emerge decades after the initial infection to cause new problems. The virus that causes chicken pox, for example, can trigger shingles many years later. And scientists have recently learned that infection with the common Epstein-Barr virus seriously increases the risk of a person developing the autoimmune disorder multiple sclerosis. "I don't think we've seen the end of this movie yet," Al-Aly says of SARS-CoV-2's long-term impacts.

Moreover, COVID has already shown its potential to cause lasting harm in the form of long COVID, which can include debilitating fatigue, breathing problems, difficulty thinking, digestive issues, and a wide variety of other symptoms. As of mid-2023 long COVID impacted 11 percent of Americans reporting a previous infection—a notable decline from the previous year. Scientists are still working to determine what triggers long COVID, but it's clear that people can develop the condition after several infections, not just their first encounter with COVID.

"Each time that you have COVID, you have a chance of having post-COVID condition afterwards," Rylance says, though he adds that "it's still fairly unpredictable at an individual level."

While scientists desperately want more data to better understand the ways COVID could shape a person's health for years to come, the hints available now are worrying, experts say. "There's a major concern here that people who are getting repeated infections [could] have long-term consequences," Nath says. "And the data that is coming out suggests that possibility."

Although COVID is now endemic and widely circulating, people and societies can both work to minimize the odds of infection, Van Kerkhove and Al-Aly say. For individuals, getting vaccinated and masking in public and crowded spaces remain the most effective strategies for avoiding COVID or reducing the severity of an infection. Unfortunately, just one in five adults in the U.S. had gotten the updated 2023-2024 COVID vaccine as of mid-January, according to the CDC—even though initial analysis of the vaccines shows that they are about 50 percent effective against infections, including by the latest subvariant, known as JN.1. Testing for COVID when feeling unwell and using antiviral medications such as Paxlovid also remain vital tools for reducing disease risk.

WHO's Van Kerkhove says that government action is key, including ensuring that masks, vaccines, tests, and treatments are available and affordable. But she also called on governments to take bolder steps such as strengthening ventilation requirements in buildings and supporting the development of better vaccines, including an oral or nasal vaccine that could more effectively prevent against COVID in the respiratory tract, where the virus enters a person's body. In addition, Al-Aly says, we need a longer-lasting vaccine that would offer meaningful protection for several years, so people would not need to get vaccinated every year.

"It's not beyond the might of U.S. medicine to really develop the technology and to deliver those solutions," Al-Aly says of such next-generation vaccines. He says the investment is particularly important now that we understand that COVID is not a problem we will dispense with quickly—and now that concerns are mounting about the damage of repeated infections.

"Those are going to be the long-term, sustainable solutions," Al-Aly says. "It isn't sustainable to ask people to mask for the next 100 years."

About the Author

Meghan Bartels is a science journalist based in New York City. She joined Scientific American *in 2023 and is now a senior news reporter there. Previously, she spent more than four years as a writer and editor at Space.com, as well as nearly a year as a science reporter at* Newsweek, *where she focused on space and Earth science. Her writing has also appeared in* Audubon, Nautilus, Astronomy *and* Smithsonian, *among other publications. She attended Georgetown University and earned a master's degree in journalism at New York University's Science, Health and Environmental Reporting Program.*

Do Repeat COVID Infections Increase the Risk of Severe Disease or Long COVID?

By Charles Schmidt

Reinfections with SARS-CoV-2, the virus that causes the disease, are on the rise, dashing hopes that vaccination or prior disease confers long-lasting immunity to infection. As more people get reinfected, they may be wondering: Do repeat infections lead to more severe COVID symptoms?

Evidence is still limited, but the available data show that while most reinfected people recover within a few days, "others are having a much rougher time," says Josh Fessel, a pulmonologist at the National Center for Advancing Translational Sciences, in Bethesda, Md. Evaluating the impacts of reinfection—especially with new viral variants arising that are successively more contagious—is an urgent priority, Fessel and other experts say.

The first study of health risks from repeat infections was published last November. A team of researchers led by Ziyad Al-Aly, a clinical epidemiologist at Washington University, in St. Louis, and his colleagues concluded that reinfected people are twice as likely to die and three times as likely to be hospitalized with COVID than those infected only once, regardless of their vaccination status. Al-Aly's team reviewed data from nearly half a million COVID patients treated by the U.S. Department of Veterans Affairs (VA) between March 2020 and April 2022. Among them, roughly 10 percent had been infected with SARS-CoV-2 between two and four times. Some patients continued to have symptoms during the six months of follow-up, Al-Aly says, and the severity of a patient's disease typically worsened with each new COVID episode.

Given those findings, Al-Aly emphasizes that repeat infections are "consequential both in the acute and long COVID phase." But his results also have important caveats: the VA patients were mostly older males, averaging 63 years in age, and many had preexisting health problems, including heart disease—all factors that can independently worsen COVID outcomes, Al-Aly says.

"This study's findings were unanticipated," says Stanley Perlman, a microbiologist at the University of Iowa's Roy J. and Lucille A. Carver College of Medicine, in Iowa City, who was not involved in the study. "We would have expected repeat disease to be milder because of immunity from the first infection." Perlman emphasizes that Al-Aly's results still need to be validated in other populations, and that more research on reinfections is needed, especially among vaccinated people exposed to newer variants. Most hospitalizations and deaths from COVID are occurring among the elderly and in unvaccinated or immunocompromised people, Perlman says. But for people outside those groups, "I think most subsequent infections are milder than the initial ones," he speculates, but he cautions that there could be unexpected immunological effects occurring that scientists do not understand.

Yet recent data reinforce Al-Aly's evidence that repeat infections can be severe, while providing new insights into what heightens risks for vulnerable people. A preprint study posted in January (which has not yet been peer-reviewed), for instance, reported that the severity of a person's initial bout with COVID predicts how severe the disease might be should it strike again. The investigators in this case reviewed electronic health records from a more diverse population of 1.5 million COVID patients treated at U.S. hospitals between March 1, 2020 and July 1, 2022. Nearly 6 percent of these individuals had been infected more than once, and in most cases, the reinfections occurred when the original Omicron variant was spreading (November 2021 to mid-March 2022).

Among those hospitalized with severe COVID the first time around, nearly half were hospitalized again when reinfected. Conversely, roughly 90 percent of people with mild initial infections avoided hospitalization when sickened again with COVID later. Notably, the investigators found that reinfections were also associated with elevated risks of long COVID—lingering symptoms such as fatigue, shortness of breath, and brain fog that persist months or years after an initial infection. But the basis for that trend is unclear. There could be biological factors at play, or maybe "doctors are simply documenting a backlog of long COVID with the new diagnostic code, which became available in late 2021," says Emily Hadley, a data scientist at RTI International, a nonprofit research institute in Durham, N.C., and the study's first author.

"It is hard to attribute a long COVID diagnosis that occurs after a reinfection to just one prior infection or to a combination of the two," adds Richard Moffitt, a bioinformatics specialist at Emory University's Winship Cancer Institute, in Atlanta, and one of Hadley's co-authors. "And it is even harder to disambiguate two distinct long-COVID diagnoses from one continuous experience."

That the severity of an initial infection would, in turn, predict the severity of future COVID episodes makes physiological sense, says Ralph Baric, a virologist at the University of North Carolina (UNC), in Chapel Hill. "Repeat infections in the heart can induce myocarditis"–inflammation of the heart–"which has the potential to [produce] blood clots," he says. "If the clots accumulate in various organs, they cause hypoxia [low oxygen in tissues] that can become a problem especially for elderly patients." Moreover, genetic risks for severe COVID and certain types of chronic lung disease, such as the lung-scarring illness pulmonary fibrosis, overlap with each other, Baric says, "and if that genetic component keeps getting stimulated by repeat infections, then you might wind up with long-term problems."

Richard Boucher, a pulmonologist at the UNC School of Medicine, agrees that people with widespread lung scarring face especially high risks from reinfection. "You worry about it in patients who had COVID and were left with severe pulmonary disease for months and months," he says. "These patients are already behind the eight ball. You don't want the virus to kick them again and add to the fibrosis they already have."

But new data also point to a promising development. SARS-CoV-2 is particularly dangerous when it settles in the lungs and causes systemic problems, such as fever, cough, and shortness of breath. Early COVID variants often invaded the lungs, yet a recently posted preprint by scientists in Japan reports that in people who are vaccinated or previously sickened with COVID, reinfection by Omicron subvariants tends to mostly affect the nose and upper airways. The antiviral immune attack generates uncomfortable symptoms, but they also tend to resolve quickly. Citing these data, Boucher says these findings help to confirm that even though vaccination will not prevent reinfection or an upper airway illness, "it can help to protect you from far more troublesome systemic infections and bad outcomes, such as the need for mechanical ventilation, or death." Moreover, since vaccines blunt the severity of initial COVID infections, by extension, they should limit the severity of future infections as well, says Moffitt.

"Reinfections are happening," Moffitt says. "Most people have had just one, but a minority of people are being reinfected multiple times, and we expect their numbers will increase."

About the Author

Charles Schmidt is a freelance journalist based in Portland, Me., covering health and the environment. He has written for Scientific American *about therapeutic viruses that can infect harmful bacteria and about dangerous contaminants in drinking water.*

Why Some People Haven't Caught COVID Despite Being Exposed

By Saima S. Iqbal

Not everyone who is exposed to SARS-CoV-2, the virus that causes COVID, gets the disease. New research published in June in *Nature* may partly explain why: In a 2021 experiment called a challenge study, researchers attempted to infect 16 unvaccinated volunteers with a low dose of the original strain of SARS-CoV-2. Participants who quickly squelched the virus activated a fast-acting innate immune response in their nose.

In the study, the team first assessed the participants' baseline immune function and then spritzed an infectious solution into their nose. For four weeks afterward, the researchers collected nasal swabs and blood samples from the subjects for single-cell DNA sequencing analysis. This offered the scientists "an unprecedented view of what happens at the very early stage of viral exposure in humans," says Akiko Iwasaki, an immunologist at the Yale School of Medicine, who was not involved in the study.

After inoculation, 6 of the 16 subjects developed a full-blown COVID infection, accompanied by mild symptoms such as a sore throat and nasal congestion. Three others tested positive or nearly positive in an on-and-off fashion but had very mild or no symptoms. These individuals' so-called transient infections were weak and short-lived. And the remaining seven participants resisted infection altogether, never testing positive.

The three people who fought off transient infections produced heavy doses of signaling proteins called interferons in their nose on day one after infection. In contrast, those who developed a full-blown infection showed interferons in their blood as early as day two but not in their nose until day five.

Interferons equip cells to defend against foreign invaders such as SARS-CoV-2: they momentarily halt major life functions that viruses hack into to replicate. A cell can produce interferons midway through an infection, before a virus has taken over its machinery, or it can trigger particular immune cells to produce the signal after it dies. Cells in the transiently infected group of participants sounded the body's alarm before SARS-CoV-2 refashioned them into virus-making factories, warding off illness. The participants with a full-blown infection responded more slowly; once their body detected infection, it went into a panic that sent interferons everywhere. As a result, interferons reached the nose—the site of infection—later than they appeared in the bloodstream, giving the virus more time to multiply.

The idea that a powerful interferon response may help people suppress COVID is unlikely to surprise immunologists. The finding lines up with previous research that linked children's relative resistance to COVID to their abnormally strong nasal innate immune responses and correlated higher levels of interferons in the blood to less severe disease. The new study underscores the important role interferons can play in defending against SARS-CoV-2 and the way that role varies throughout the body over the course of an infection.

Researchers do not yet understand why some people more quickly rally the innate immune system to fight off infection or how others totally repel the virus, but genetics may play a role. In the recent study, participants who snuffed out the virus relatively early or avoided infection tended to have high levels of baseline activity in a gene called *HLA-DQA2*. The gene produces a type of protein known to present immune cells with snippets of foreign invaders. It's unclear whether the protein's activity makes a person resilient to infection or is merely a product of an effective immune response, however. "We can't really distinguish the chicken and the egg here," says Rik Lindeboom, co-lead author of the study and a researcher at the Netherlands Cancer Institute.

How quickly an infected person pumps out interferons may not matter as much these days, when most people have already been infected with the virus or vaccinated against it, Iwasaki says. The body's adaptive immune response—its slower, pathogen-specific defense—will likely come to the rescue if the innate response is slow. And some strains of the virus appear to have developed defense mechanisms against the interferon response, blunting its effect.

A case still remains for using interferon-boosting agents as a supplemental therapy, if timed well, Iwasaki notes. The challenge study makes clear that in order to effectively prevent infection, interferon levels must peak at or before day one. That means any potential drug would function best as a preventive measure—taken, say, before attending a concert—or as a "plan B" medication post-exposure. Some clinical trials have implemented these therapies past that time window, however, producing mixed results.

Companies could also use data from the infected participants to create better COVID vaccines, Lindeboom says. They could gauge their vaccines' effectiveness by comparing the responses of immune cells called T cells to vaccination with the T cell responses seen in people who are recovering from COVID. And new nasal vaccines in development aim to block infection at the start by eliciting an adaptive immune response in the nose rather than the circulatory system.

Some people have interpreted the powerful capacity of the innate immune response as a reason to dismiss vaccines, he adds, but the response differs among individuals and cannot provide complete protection from the virus. Yet even mild COVID infections raise a person's risk of heart problems and long COVID; widespread inflammation caused by a systemic immune response puts stress on the body's organs.

The participants in the new study did not—thankfully—experience any long-term side effects, at least for up to one year post-exposure. But vaccination remains the most surefire way to limit both infection and long-term illness.

About the Author

Saima S. Iqbal is Scientific American's *current news intern. She specializes in health and medicine and is based in New York City.*

What Is Paxlovid Rebound, and How Common Is It?

By Fionna M. D. Samuels

When President Joe Biden was diagnosed with COVID, he started taking an oral treatment of the antiviral Paxlovid almost immediately. Four days after finishing the Paxlovid regime and testing negative, however, Biden once again tested positive for COVID—but without any symptoms of the disease. This is perhaps the highest-profile example of what people are calling "Paxlovid rebound." Anthony Fauci, the president's chief medical advisor, also experienced it. This condition has been reported in a minority of people who have received the antiviral and remains an active area of research.

Scientific American spoke with infectious disease experts about what the phenomenon is, how common it might be, and what people should do if they get it.

What is Paxlovid?

Paxlovid is an oral, three-pill antiviral regimen taken daily for five days. The drug, made by Pfizer, is prescribed to people who catch COVID and are at risk of severe disease. This can include those who are unvaccinated or elderly or have other medical conditions ranging from diabetes to cancer. Two of the three pills are nirmatrelvir, a drug that targets enzymes specific to the COVID-causing virus and suppresses replication. The third pill is ritonavir, a drug first developed to help treat HIV/AIDS, which boosts the level of the first medication by slowing its breakdown in the body.

"Everything that we've done for COVID came out of the HIV playbook, just flat out," says Davey Smith, the head of infectious diseases and global public health at the University of California, San Diego. That includes "the development of vaccines, the development of treatments, how we did the testing, how we did epidemiology," he says.

Clinical trials showed Paxlovid was extremely successful at reducing severe disease. In the group that received the drug, it cut COVID hospitalizations and deaths by 89 percent compared to those who received a placebo sugar pill.

To help people gain access to the lifesaving drug, the Biden-Harris administration rolled out a Test to Treat program so that anyone can be tested for COVID and receive Paxlovid in one trip to a pharmacy or treatment center.

What is Paxlovid rebound?

The CDC defines Paxlovid rebound as when a patient who, after receiving a full five-day course of treatment, either has a reemergence of COVID symptoms or tests positive after a previous, negative test. Under this classification, when you rebound, "you can have virus without symptoms, symptoms without virus, and you can have the two together," Smith says. He adds that he's slightly annoyed by the blanket classification of "rebound" because in virology, a "rebound" is when there is a reemergence of measurable amounts of virus.

The Pfizer clinical trial reported between 1 and 2 percent of those who received the drug tested positive for COVID after finishing the Paxlovid course; their illness rebounded. Those rebounds were not statistically different from rebounds experienced by people with COVID who received the placebo, however.

"From a research definition, the reemergence of symptoms with a positive test is 'symptomatic [Paxlovid] rebound,'" says Amy Barczak, an infectious disease doctor at Massachusetts General Hospital and COVID researcher. "A positive test and the absence of symptoms–which nobody is looking for–that would be 'asymptomatic Paxlovid rebound.' " The latter is what Biden has, and was detected because he was testing daily.

Adi Shah, an infectious disease specialist at the Mayo Clinic in Minnesota, explains that another complicating factor he considers in patients is differentiating between a true rebound of symptoms and just a very slow improvement in symptoms after starting Paxlovid. Clinically, this is a vital distinction because it can change how people are deciding to isolate. These differences also have ramifications for research; to accurately say how many people experience Paxlovid rebound, it needs to be correctly identified.

It's important to remember that "if your patient needs it, the drug works, even in the setting of some people [having] rebound," Smith says. "The clinical trials were very clear that this was a great drug to keep people out of hospital and from dying. So don't be scared of the rebound."

Who is experiencing Paxlovid rebound, and how common is it?

"In our [work], being of an elderly age and then having other risk factors–like diabetes, heart disease, kidney disease, or some sort of cancer–does put you at a higher risk of rebound," says Shah. Many of these are the same as the risk factors for severe COVID.

Unfortunately, as previously noted, it's difficult to know exactly how frequently Paxlovid rebound occurs because "rebound" needs to be uniformly defined first. Barczak explains that if rebound is sometimes classified as only a reoccurrence of symptoms and other times classified as having multiple negative tests followed by multiple positive tests, this could change the percentage of people thought to be experiencing the phenomenon. Regardless, she still estimates rebound associated with reemergence of the virus to be higher than what was reported in the original Pfizer clinical trials. "What we say is, somewhere between 2 and 10 percent [of people taking Paxlovid experience rebound]," she says. "I think it's probably somewhere in that range, but I don't [know] precisely."

In a recently published retrospective review of Mayo Clinic patients, Shah found that about 1 percent of Paxlovid users rebounded, which is consistent with the Pfizer clinical trial. But based on discussions he has since had with patients and other physicians, "I think the actual rate might be high as high as 5 to 10 percent," he says.

Shah says that, right now, it is difficult to nail down exactly how many people may be experiencing a rebound because "you need real documentation of three tests–a positive, a negative, a positive–and clear documentation of symptoms–all symptoms gone, symptoms come back." This is challenging to do retrospectively because clinics need to have already collected all that information, and it is challenging to do prospectively because patients may not know they have rebounded so are not testing themselves for COVID, or they may not tell anyone they have rebounded.

Barzcak points out that it's only recently that doctors and researchers have started enrolling Paxlovid users in studies of rebound. "It takes a while to actually enroll people in these prospective studies," she explains. Once the results of those studies are published, scientists will likely have a better idea of how many people actually experience the phenomenon.

What should you do if you have Paxlovid rebound?

"I want to emphasize that the good thing is, even if you have rebound, outcomes are good," Shah says. In general, "you're not needing additional COVID therapies, you're not needing hospitalization, and you're not experiencing high mortality or morbidity."

However, it is still important to isolate after a rebound. "I think it's very likely that a subset of individuals–probably not everybody, but a subset of individuals with rebound symptoms after Paxlovid–are newly infectious during that time of rebound," Barczak says. She and her team took nasal samples from seven individuals experiencing rebound symptoms and were able to culture virus from three people, suggesting those individuals could infect others. Despite this study's tiny sample size, "people need to be aware that they may be infectious," she says. "If your symptoms come back, think about protecting the people around you, and isolate, mask and test."

In addition to isolating and masking up, it is important to tell your doctor that you are, once again, experiencing symptoms of COVID. "People who are in certain types of chemotherapy and [those with] certain immunosuppressed conditions," Smith says, "really need to talk to the doctor about that," because they are at the highest risk for severe disease. These are the people Smith usually treats for rebound with a second course of Paxlovid–just as Fauci was.

For others, he tells them to stay home and isolate because "there's no reason to go around and spread it." Some experts disagree that a second course of Paxlovid is warranted for rebound cases.

What causes Paxlovid rebound?

Rebound may occur because some patients are not receiving high enough doses of nirmatrelvir, the part of Paxlovid that targets COVID enzymes. That dose already needs to be boosted in the body, which is why ritonavir is part of the treatment regime. Smith's own research found that rebound was not a result of the virus becoming resistant to the drug. He hypothesizes that people in the "real world" might decide to skip a dose because Paxlovid can make food taste bad. Or those who rebound may be part of the minority of people who don't experience the right rate of drug release with the combination of nirmatrelvir and ritonavir. Either way, experiencing a lower dose could lead to pockets of virus surviving through the treatment and then reemerging days later. Smith thinks that ongoing research really needs to focus on the idea that some patients may not be exposed to the correct dosage of Paxlovid.

As scientists continue to learn more about Paxlovid rebound, all the doctors *Scientific American* spoke with emphasized that they will continue to prescribe Paxlovid to their patients who need it. "We can still use Paxlovid effectively," Barczak says. "And we can protect one another by masking and testing and isolating when rebound happens."

About the Author

Fionna M. D. Samuels was a 2022 AAAS Mass Media Fellow at Scientific American. *She's pursuing a Ph.D. in chemistry at Colorado State University. Follow her on X (formerly Twitter) @Fairy__Hedgehog.*

Why Some People Get Sick More Often

By Elana Spivack

Everyone gets sick. Despite all the vegetables we eat or vitamins we gulp down, sooner or later pathogens such as viruses and harmful bacteria infiltrate our bodies, and we need to take a time-out. We sit back and let our immune system do its job.

But when it comes to getting sick, not all immune systems are equal. Some people seem to get sick much more often than others. One could easily conclude that these individuals—such as elementary school teachers or hospital workers—are merely exposed to sick people more often. But susceptibility to illness isn't as simple as the odds of being exposed to someone with a cold. Each person gets sick differently.

Moreover, people recover differently. Not everyone returns to their baseline level of health after the flu or COVID. The biology behind why and how some people get sick more often than others is still largely unknown. But a paper published on June 13 in *Nature Communications* shines a light on the components of immune resilience—the ability to restore immune functions that stave off diseases and control inflammation caused by infectious diseases, as well as other sources of inflammation.

Scientific American spoke with the study's lead author, Sunil Ahuja, a professor of medicine at the University of Texas Health Science Center at San Antonio and director of the Department of Veterans Affairs Center for Personalized Medicine, about why some people fall ill more often.

[An edited transcript of the interview follows.]

Q: Why are some people more susceptible to getting sick?

A: In general, one would consider three main factors. One would be genetic susceptibility: you're born with a genetic predisposition to becoming infected more easily. You could have inborn errors, such as polymorphisms in genes that are well described for host immunity.

Second would be environments where there's a heavy burden of infection. If you look at our ancestors, a lot of them passed away by the time they were in their 50s because they had a greater antigenic load [the amount of inflammatory stress an infection causes] before there were vaccines, higher living standards, and better sanitation.

These are kind of static factors. But then the third factor is response to inflammatory stress. I might respond in one way to one infection and in another way to a different infection. It's a yin-yang. Environment plays a role, and that same genetic thing that's protective against one infection can be detrimental for another infection. People show variation in how they respond to these challenges–which could also have a genetic basis. When we respond to challenges, we all have what I would call "a burst of inflammation." We all need some inflammation, but it has to be the right amount at the right place at the right time. The injured or infected site gets swollen, red, and warm. These signs of inflammation at that site are saying, "Help, I need white blood cells to show up at that site to ward off further spread of this inflammation and to allow for healing." The body produces these chemical substances, which we now call chemokines. "Chemo" stands for "chemoattractant"–it's the attractant for white blood cells.

There are people who can be hyperinflamed and hypoinflamed. People vary in their amount of inflammation. In our study, being able to control inflammation and preserve immunocompetence was associated with being asymptomatic. Some people are infected yet don't get sick because they had a really good inflammatory response.

Q: It seems that people in some professions, such as teachers, get sick more often. Why is that?

A: One reason is in part related to the microbial load. You're taking 30 or 40 kids into close quarters. It's exposure. Not everyone will get sick. It's a subgroup of these people. This susceptibility is population-based, not individual-based. If I took a group of day-care workers, they have so much exposure to respiratory viruses, influenza, and so on. The greater the exposure, the greater the likelihood there will be some degradation.

I told you about inflammation and how it can increase or decrease an effective immune response. We go through such cycles repeatedly in our life. There will be some people who, despite these repeated cycles, manage to preserve that resilience piece; there will be some people whose response is moderately degraded; and there will be some people who have this susceptibility at any age to degrade—that's what we call nonoptimal.

The traditional way of doing research is to compare the old versus the young. This presumes that the only thing that is different between a young person and an old person is their age when, in fact, that's not quite true. One might need to break down the old group into varying degrees of immune health. That'd be like saying, "I'm in my 60s"—which I am—"and I'm now an old fart, and I'm like every other old fart." That may not be true. There are old farts who are 110 years old who do just fine.

As a whole, a group may be at greater risk of getting infections, but that risk is largely localized to those people with eroded immune health. Among that group is a subset who are susceptible to degraded immune resilience—that is, among people of a similar age. We know that as one grows older, one's immunocompetence declines. So these infections tend to degrade our immune health at any age.

Q: How can immune resilience affect a person's longevity?

A: We could categorize people into four groups. People who have high immunocompetence and low inflammation—by definition, the most protected group–live longer. Then you have those with low immunocompetence and high inflammation. These people will, unfortunately, after controlling for age, die sooner than others. Those who have high immunocompetence, which is good, coupled with high inflammation, which is bad, have an intermediate life span. So do those who have low immunocompetence and low inflammation.

I want to give you an example of those cycles, such as in people who have had a natural influenza infection. Temporarily, they turned on so-called mortality-associated biomarkers. Over time, there was a recovery process. We have these injury-repair cycles. If people have too much injury and not enough repair, they will have some residual inflammation. They got hit with influenza, and then, over time, they recovered, but there was a small group who had this residual stuff left behind.

Q: Are there ways to prevent an infection from seriously harming you?

A: That would be analogous to saying, "Can I be certain that when I go to my grocery store, some idiot does not want to kill me?" So I don't think so. Some of the fittest people have gotten the flu and passed away. Among people who have good immune health, can I predict a priori that they will do as well during an infection? I cannot predict that. That is the problem. We do know that people, even young people, who have poor immune health don't do so well after a vaccine. I could advise them that there is a chance that they may not do so well after getting vaccinated because of their immune health score.

I can only tell you ways to possibly prevent exposure risks that could potentially protect you.

Q: How can you reduce your risk of getting exposed to pathogens?

A: I'm still very pleased when I see older veterans walking into the hospital with a mask on because it tells me they still understand the basic principle that their immune health is poor, or they've been informed of it, and they protect themselves.

Your diet and, I suspect, most importantly, exercise also play a role. I suspect that people who maintain regular sustained exercise, not just periodic exercise, are afforded immune benefits. There's a huge behavioral component to all of this to change human behavior to mitigate risk. I think behavioral change is so difficult.

The two major things that I would focus on are to use common sense precautions and to address behavioral issues.

About the Author

Elana Spivack is a science journalist in New York City who covers reproductive health, food science, and more. Follow her on X (formerly Twitter) @ElanaSpivack.

Section 3: Scientific Breakthroughs

A High-Speed Scientific Hive Mind Emerged from the COVID Pandemic

By Joseph Bak-Coleman & Carl T. Bergstrom

Most of the time science is a slow and tedious business. Researchers toil away for decades at obscure limits of human knowledge, collecting and analyzing data, refining theories, writing, debating, and advancing our understanding of the world in tiny increments. Working in small teams on highly specialized projects far from the public eye—that is what most of us are accustomed to doing.

But a calamity upends everything. In early 2020 COVID spread around the globe. Millions of lives were at stake. Yet we knew next to nothing about the nature of the threat. Just a few months earlier no one had ever seen the SARS-CoV-2 virus.

For researchers, the emergence of the disease was an all-hands-on-deck moment. Biologists such as the two of us, along with virologists and immunologists, all pivoted to focus on the new pathogen. And other researchers from across the scientific ecosystem—economists, physicists, engineers, statisticians, psychologists, sociologists, and more—dropped everything to learn about COVID and figure out how they could contribute. Public interest exploded. Scientists with scant experience in public communication learned to work closely with journalists, informing a worried public about what was happening, what to expect next and what people could do to keep themselves safe. The scale of cooperation and collaboration is staggering. Large-scale surveys of scientists done in 2020 and 2021 show that roughly a third of researchers in the U.S. and Europe contributed to the effort.

This vast collaboration moved quickly and effectively in several areas. On December 30, 2019, an epidemiological surveillance network published the first English-language note about a cluster of pneumonia cases of unknown cause in Wuhan, China. Eight days later Chinese scientists identified the pathogen as a novel coronavirus. The full genome sequence was published just two days after that. Then on January 13, 2020, the World Health Organization published instructions for a PCR-based diagnostic test based on that genome.

The genome sequence also opened the door for vaccine development. Scientists used it to determine the 3-D structure of the SARS-CoV-2 spike protein, and by the end of January they had figured out how to stabilize the protein to make it an effective vaccine component, leading to mRNA-based and other vaccines, which were developed, tested, and distributed in less than a year.

The urgency of COVID drove scientists to adapt. Discussions that previously took place at conferences, on the telephone or in revision notes on manuscripts moved to social media platforms such as Twitter, review sites such as PubPeer and all-hours Zoom rooms. Researchers and clinicians spontaneously organized into focused teams and working groups. By rapidly sharing information on their patients, physicians figured out that people with severe COVID were at high risk for dangerous blood clots in their lungs, so anticoagulants became a standard of care and saved lives.

In general, traditional modes of publication were far too slow. We embraced a rapid alternative model: preprint archives, where papers are posted prior to peer review or consideration at a scientific journal. The number of papers submitted to medRxiv, a key repository of biomedical preprints, increased 10-fold in the first few months of the pandemic.

These changes also shifted early-stage science from a private activity to part of the public discourse. Instead of presenting the world with polished scientific articles, investigators worked in open view, thinking aloud, offering preliminary speculations, arguing, making wrong turns, following dead ends and pursuing some hypotheses that would ultimately be refuted.

This approach to communication does have a downside. Previously private communications were now open to exploitation and distortion by politicians and pundits. For instance, flawed blood-sample research reported in an April 2020 medRxiv paper purported to show that COVID was a mild disease with a very low fatality rate. Although the scientific community quickly pointed out a host of problems with the work, people seeking to avoid business restrictions, school closures, and mask mandates ignored the criticism and used the paper to undermine public health interventions.

Rapid and unorthodox channels of communication also could not solve all the problems scientists encountered. We took too long to recognize the importance of airborne transmission of the virus. We spent early 2020 washing our groceries but not wearing masks. Most critically, we have been largely unsuccessful at anticipating and managing the human element of the pandemic. By not accounting for ways that behavior would change in response to information—and misinformation—we have struggled to predict the size and timing of successive disease waves and virus variants. A collective failure to stop misinformation from spreading on social and traditional media platforms has left large segments of the population unvaccinated, vulnerable, and unwilling to embrace measures such as masks and social distancing.

By some measures COVID has also hampered scientific productivity overall, researchers suggested in a paper in *Nature Communications* late last year. Some of the 2020 survey data revealed that scientists were spending an average of seven fewer hours per week working on research. The group, led by Dashun Wang of Northwestern University, wrote that the decrease in productivity will likely have lasting effects, with scientists reporting fewer publications, collaborations, submitted papers, and new projects started during the pandemic. Lockdowns, school closures and other changes took a disproportionate toll on women scientists juggling work and child care—a major problem that requires urgent redress.

But a publication dip is precisely what we would expect when scientists shift from day-to-day research to an emergency response. Placing papers in journals becomes secondary to fixing problems. Dealing with urgent issues is one of the most important roles of the publicly funded scientific ecosystem, which has millions of researchers effectively on retainer. When global crises arise, they organize, learn, and coordinate. And that, ultimately, leads to solutions.

About the Authors

Joseph Bak-Coleman is a postdoctoral fellow at the University of Washington Center for an Informed Public. He studies how communications technology affects collective decision-making.

Carl T. Bergstrom is a professor in the department of biology and a faculty member at the Center for an Informed Public at the University of Washington. Over the past decade, he has written numerous scholarly articles on the spread of misinformation. He is co-author of the undergraduate textbook Evolution *and of* Calling Bullshit: The Art of Skepticism in a Data-Driven World.

Five Things We've Learned from COVID in Three Years

By Stephanie Pappas

Three years ago, on March 11, 2020, Tedros Adhanom Ghebreyesus, director general of the World Health Organization (WHO), announced that the coronavirus that causes COVID was spreading worldwide and that the outbreak was officially a pandemic. At the time, there were more than 118,000 confirmed cases of COVID and 4,291 official deaths.

"In the days and weeks ahead," Ghebreyesus said in a press conference at the time, "we expect to see the number of cases, the number of deaths and the number of affected countries climb even higher."

Three years later the WHO has recorded more than 6.8 million COVID deaths, though studies of global excess mortality, or deaths above and beyond the expected amount in a given time, suggest the actual number is more than double that amount. In the U.S., there have been an estimated 1.1 million deaths from COVID, according to the U.S. Centers for Disease Control and Prevention. Long COVID, which occurs when people experience lingering or new symptoms even after recovering from the initial infection, has also emerged as a threat that is still mysterious, though doctors are increasingly honing in on possible causes and treatments.

The most at-risk populations now are individuals with preexisting chronic illnesses whose health is fragile and for whom hospitalization is a regular occurrence, says Jeremy Faust, an emergency medicine physician at Brigham and Women's Hospital in Boston. COVID is one more factor that can push those individuals toward death. As a result, the pandemic is still causing excess mortality in the U.S. Mortality fluctuates from month to month but was approximately 10 percent higher in November 2022 than it was prepandemic, Faust says.

If March 2020 was like a flood, Faust says, today the world is no longer drowning. But the new normal is just a bit worse than before, he says: "Sea level is just higher," Faust adds.

There is greater awareness now that a pandemic virus can rock societies, says Amesh Adalja, an infectious disease physician and senior scholar at the Johns Hopkins Center for Health Security. That awareness has not always translated to action, however. "It's still not highly prioritized by policy makers, and there are really big questions about how the U.S. could respond" to a future pandemic, Adalja says. Public health missteps in the 2022–2023 monkeypox outbreak, ranging from poor access to testing to clumsy vaccine distribution, echoed those early in the COVID pandemic, he says.

"Until [infectious disease] is prioritized in a way that national security is, I don't think you're going to see full resilience," Adalja says. "What you need is a proactive, sustained approach that doesn't just last an election cycle."

Despite the challenges of building preparedness, we have learned some hard-won lessons about SARS-CoV-2, the coronavirus that causes COVID, that could inform our approach to future pandemics—and public health in general.

mRNA Vaccines Are Safe, Powerful, and Effective

One of the unambiguous successes of the response to the COVID pandemic was the rapid development of effective vaccines.

The pandemic was the first large-scale test for mRNA vaccine technology, which proved safe and effective against severe disease and death even as the virus evolved to form new variants. A recent analysis by the Commonwealth Fund, an independent research group that focuses on health-care issues, found that in the two years after vaccines were introduced in the U.S., the shots prevented an estimated 18 million hospitalizations and three million deaths.

Masks Work

Masks and mask mandates became a political flashpoint during the pandemic, but the evidence shows that they slow the spread of COVID and other respiratory illnesses. For instance, according to the CDC, at least 10 studies as of late 2021 found that after local authorities implemented universal masking mandates, infection rates declined.

The best protection comes from high-quality N95 and KN95 masks. An influential publication in February 2022 in the CDC's *Morbidity and Mortality Weekly Report* compared people who had tested positive for COVID and people who had not and assessed their mask-wearing habits. Among 534 participants who reported their mask type, a consistent cloth mask usage lowered the odds of testing positive by 56 percent, surgical mask wearing lowered the odds by 66 percent, and N95 or KN95 usage lowered the odds by 83 percent. Masks are most effective when they are sealed well, worn correctly, and layered with other precautions.

Indoor Air Quality Matters

In early 2020 no one knew how the virus spread, and the CDC and other health agencies around the world were sending out mixed messages. Hand sanitizer became a national obsession. People wiped down their groceries or left them overnight in their garage.

But research would soon confirm that the virus primarily spread through the air rather than via surfaces. This realization has triggered an interest in improving indoor air quality through both ventilation (letting outside air in) and filtration (cleaning the air of particles and pathogens). Research has found that continuous high-efficiency particulate air (HEPA) filtration can remove the vast majority of COVID viral particles in the air and dramatically lower exposure. And the effect isn't limited to COVID: filtration removes other viral particles such as flu from the air, too.

Wastewater Tracking is Useful for COVID and Other Diseases

The idea to track viral spread through wastewater first arose early in 2020 and has now become a national program. Wastewater has provided up to several weeks' warning of coming viral surges because people begin to shed SARS-CoV-2 before they feel symptoms or seek medical care. Wastewater tracking is now integrated into other disease surveillance. Scientists have used sewage to track surges of viruses such as RSV and influenza.

Genomic Surveillance is Key for Tracking Viral Evolution

SARS-CoV-2 does not remain static. Over the past three years, variants such as Delta, which caused a surge of disease and severe illness in 2021, and the extremely transmissible Omicron, which spread rapidly in late 2021 and is still the dominant variant worldwide, have changed the course of the pandemic. Variants rise and fall in dominance as they outcompete one another to spread through the population, though Omicron subvariants currently make up 99.9 percent of all cases.

Countries and health agencies around the world have now established genomic surveillance to track novel concerning variants. Strong surveillance is key to responding to new pandemic twists and turns, according to Jarbas Barbosa, director of the Pan American Health Organization, which coordinates a regional genomic surveillance network in the Americas. The challenge is to maintain interest in these efforts even as the acute phase of the pandemic recedes.

"As we learn to live with this virus, countries must ... maintain and continue to strengthen surveillance," Barbosa said a media briefing on March 9. "The risk of new variants is real."

About the Author

Stephanie Pappas is a freelance science journalist based in Denver, Colo.

Scientists Behind mRNA COVID Vaccines Win 2023 Nobel Prize in Physiology or Medicine

By Lauren J. Young

This year's Nobel Prize in Physiology or Medicine goes to a transformative medical technology that significantly altered the path of the pandemic and saved millions: the mRNA vaccines against COVID. Katalin Karikó and Drew Weissman were jointly awarded the prize for advancements that have changed the field of vaccine development and researchers' understanding of how messenger RNA (mRNA) interacts with the body's immune system.

Speaking to *Scientific American*, Weissman describes the rollercoaster of emotions he went through after learning of the news this morning. "I'm going through a series of steps, it started off just incredible enjoyment and surprise," he says. "And right now I'm pretty much numb."

Karikó and Weissman began studying in vitro synthetic mRNA technology in the 1990s, when they worked together at the University of Pennsylvania. The pair's seminal paper in 2005 described how they were able to successfully deliver modified mRNA into the body and trigger an immune response—the kind that trains the immune system for future viral infections. Over the years, their research with mRNA vaccines solved some of the major issues confronting the technique, such as the inflammatory response by the body that involves the production of harmful cytokines. During the pandemic, this mRNA technology led to the production of highly effective vaccines against SARS-CoV-2, the COVID-causing virus, and particularly ones that were adaptable for large-scale rollout.

"What's important here I think is that vaccines could be developed so fast," said Gunilla Karlsson Hedestam, a member of the 2023 Nobel Committee for Physiology or Medicine, at this morning's announcement. This was "largely due to ... improvements in the technology and this basic discovery."

Karikó was born in 1955 in Szolnok, Hungary. In 1989 she became an assistant professor at the University of Pennsylvania, where she remained until 2013. She was a senior vice president at BioNTech RNA Pharmaceuticals–a major manufacturer of an mRNA COVID vaccine–and is now an external consultant for BioNTech. She is also a professor at the University of Szeged in Hungary and an adjunct professor at the Perelman School of Medicine at the University of Pennsylvania.

Weissman was born in 1959 in Lexington, Mass. In 1997 he established his research group at the Perelman School of Medicine. Weissman is Roberts Family Professor in Vaccine Research at the University of Pennsylvania and director of the Penn Institute for RNA Innovation.

"The award, to me, is really a victory for vaccines and the potential for vaccines to advance health and improve equity," says Kathleen Neuzil, a vaccinology professor and director of the Center for Vaccine Development and Global Health at the University of Maryland School of Medicine.

Many vaccines had been created with weakened or deactivated whole viruses, but in recent decades many researchers have been investigating smaller viral parts, such as viral genetic material: DNA or RNA. When Karikó and Weissman injected the foreign in vitro mRNA into human cells, they found that it created a strong immune reaction that elevated protective antibodies. Subsequent inflammation, as well as enzymes in human blood and cells, would degrade the mRNA, however. Despite these scientific roadblocks, skepticism and difficulties with funding, Karikó and Weissman continued to search for solutions.

"It was nonstop technical hurdles for 25 years," Weissman reflects. "We couldn't get funding, Kati [Karikó] kept getting demoted and pushed out. It was very difficult to do this research, but we saw early on the potential and how important RNA was likely to be. And that kept us going. We never gave up."

The team found a way to modify mRNA to be less inflammatory—replacing uridine, one of its building block molecules, with a similar molecule called pseudouridine. They also developed a more efficient delivery system that used lipid nanoparticles to protect the mRNA and help it to enter cells for protein production.

"In the early days of vaccinology, we would take a bacteria, we would take a virus, and we would weaken it, or we would combine it with another antigen. But here this was really a targeted immune system approach, both from the use of the mRNA and the use of the lipid nanoparticle," Neuzil says. "So, to me, that was quite impressive—that they took an entirely different approach to vaccine delivery."

Starting in the early 2000s, Karikó and Weissman conducted several animal trials with mRNA vaccines for a variety of different pathogens such as Zika, influenza, and HIV. "In every animal model we looked at, HIV was the only one that didn't work well," Weissman says. "Just about every single one of them gave us 100 percent protection."

The research unlocked a new path for possible therapy and vaccine development—one that would prove critical during the COVID pandemic.

Adapting for a Global Public Health Emergency

When SARS-CoV-2 began to spread worldwide, Weissman and Karikó's mRNA research quickly became a candidate and basis for vaccines against the virus. The mRNA vaccine approach had several advantages, Weissman explains. Only a sequence of the original pathogen was needed rather than an actual piece or full virus. "There's no growing a virus and inactivating it. It's a very simple procedure, and that's because it's a simple enzymatic reaction," Weissman says. "It was two months from the sequence being released to the first patients getting the vaccine."

Clinical trials, production, and rollout of the vaccines greatly expanded, with companies creating hundreds of millions of doses within a year. "Switching over to COVID, it was just a technical thing," Karikó told *Scientific American* in a 2021 interview. "It was already ready."

The mRNA COVID vaccines work by injecting the genetic material specifically for SARS-CoV-2's spike proteins—surface proteins on the virus that allow it to bind to healthy cells. Modified mRNA in the vaccine is taken by cells, which then decode it and produce those spike proteins so that the immune system can better identify and neutralize the real virus in the event of a future infection.

"We're coming off the worst pandemic in more than a century, and certainly these vaccines contributed to lives saved and to less morbidity," says Neuzil, who has also been working on mRNA vaccines for malaria. "I think an adaptation of this technology and mRNA vaccines could really be transformative, particularly for low- and middle-income countries, because of the adaptability and flexibility of the platform."

Future Therapies

For future vaccines, the application can be quite broad, Weissman says. When Karikó first became interested in mRNA research, she wasn't initially seeking to develop vaccines. "I was making this modification in the RNA because I always wanted to develop it for therapies," she told *Scientific American* in 2021.

While the mRNA technology has helped to tackle the COVID pandemic, a tremendous number of people will benefit from the technology, says Niek Sanders, a principal investigator at Ghent University's Laboratory of Gene Therapy in Belgium. "It can also be used to treat any disease that is due to a malfunctioning protein as it allows patients to produce their own therapeutic proteins," Sanders says. "Nobel Prizes with such a high impact on society are rare and occur only once in 25 or 50 years."

Weissman, Karikó, and other research groups are already trying to apply the technology to autoimmune diseases, cancers, food and environmental allergies, bacterial diseases, and insect-borne diseases.

In July Weissman and his colleagues published a paper in *Science* that showed they could deliver RNA gene-editing machinery directly to bone marrow stem cells. This could be key for treating diseases such as sickle cell anemia, in which stem cells are typically taken from an individual, cultured and treated, and then put back into the body. "Now we can give them an off-the-shelf injection of RNA and cure their disease, and that has applicability to thousands of other bone marrow diseases. And then you can expand that to liver, to lung, to brain, to every other organ therapeutics," Weissman says. "The potential is just enormous."

Weissman hopes that the mRNA treatment will be available to sickle cell anemia patients in a year and a half. He also has many mRNA clinical trials underway, including a phase 1 trial for the disease amyloidosis and vaccine trials for HIV, norovirus, and malaria. Wiessman's team is also planning to start clinical trials soon on a pan-coronavirus mRNA vaccine, which could help prevent future coronavirus epidemics.

"The future is now," Weissman says. "These therapeutics are in people right now."

About the Author

Lauren J. Young is an associate editor for health and medicine at Scientific American. *She has edited and written stories that tackle a wide range of subjects, including the COVID pandemic, emerging diseases, evolutionary biology and health inequities. Young has nearly a decade of newsroom and science journalism experience. Before joining* Scientific American *in 2023, she was an associate editor at* Popular Science *and a digital producer at public radio's* Science Friday. *She has appeared as a guest on radio shows, podcasts and stage events. Young has also spoken on panels for the Asian American Journalists Association, American Library Association, NOVA Science Studio and the New York Botanical Garden. Her work has appeared in* Scholastic MATH, School Library Journal, IEEE Spectrum, *Atlas Obscura and* Smithsonian Magazine. *Young studied biology at California Polytechnic State University, San Luis Obispo, before pursuing a master's at New York University's Science, Health & Environmental Reporting Program.*

How COVID Changed Science

By William A. Haseltine

Rarely in recent memory has the world faced such an immediate and widespread global threat as complex as COVID-19. In its face, a select few have risen to the occasion, none more cherished and admired perhaps than the health-care workers staffing the front lines. But standing close behind them in the trenches are the scientists and researchers who are among the very few who truly understand the scope of our evolutionary battle with the virus. Since the start of the pandemic, our scientists have acted with unprecedented speed and coordinated action to deliver us an armamentarium of medical weaponry to confront this global threat.

For someone who has spent a lifetime in science, someone who understands the pressures and constraints faced each day in every lab, it has been phenomenal to witness the transformation that has taken place within the scientific community. It is not just the speed and focus with which the scientific community responded, nor simply the use of new technologies to draw out new discoveries, but rather the singular willingness of scientists, all over the world, to share new ideas and data immediately and transparently, in some cases well before the idea or the research is fully formed.

Within weeks of the first case of COVID being reported, Chinese researchers had identified the virus they suspected of causing the disease and had decoded an initial genome sequence. It was a remarkable achievement in such a short amount of time, made more remarkable by the fact that the researchers published the sequence in an open discussion forum online, and encouraged a fellow researcher in Sydney, Australia, to share it via Twitter with the world.

During the first 24 hours after publication, an evolutionary biologist in Scotland had figured out the similarities between this virus and SARS-CoV-1 and, like the Chinese researchers, shared the findings immediately online. A researcher in the U.S. openly published the new virus' phylogenetic tree. And another started reverse-engineering a live virus from the sequence, letting colleagues around the world know that the first steps towards developing an antibody test were already underway. At each moment, the goal was not acclaim or attention, but rather the possibility that openly sharing an early finding may influence the work of others and inch the world ever closer to a treatment or a cure.

Of all the arenas in life that COVID has upended, science is perhaps the field that has been transformed the most. The pandemic has created an entirely new research environment, one that is now structured for collaboration and communication above all else. This revolution was inspired by the initial transparency of those early researchers but has since been institutionalized by some of the most well-respected research institutes in the world today, including our very own biomedical nerve center in Boston.

Shortly after the virus emerged, Harvard Medical School pulled 20 Boston-area universities, medical schools, and research institutes together to launch the Massachusetts Consortium on Pathogen Readiness (MassCPR). The initial goal was to formally join forces with researchers in China to answer the call to action to take down the emerging threat, with the hope that any lessons learned from this outbreak would enable a more rapid response to future emergencies.

This alone was a notable step. The scientific community in Boston typically works in relatively isolated fashion, with barriers built up between departments, disciplines and entire institutions. But with COVID-19 and MassCPR those floodgates between institutes upriver and down were quickly opened.

With a collaborative research grant from the Evergrande Group, MassCPR began funding dozens of new research projects, some of which have led to field-defining studies on the epidemiology, pathogenesis, and immunopathology of COVID-19. Over the past year, MassCPR clinicians have written clinical management guidelines that have influenced patient care across the globe, and the consortium's investigators have conceptualized, designed, and developed the single-dose Johnson & Johnson vaccine and spearheaded clinical trials for the Moderna one.

The dean of Harvard Medical School, George Daley, leads the effort, along with Arlene Sharpe, Bruce Walker and David Golan. As Daley describes it, "Our collective efforts over the last year have given us demonstrable proof that we are strongest when we work together across institutional boundaries, when we reach out across geographic and national borders. We are strongest when we transcend scientific silos and build bridges across disciplines. Cooperation to confront a common threat is what MassCPR represents, and the achievements speak for themselves."

MassCPR's immediate efforts are focused on the basic biology of SARS-CoV-2 and the pathogenesis of COVID-19—developing new diagnostic tools, vaccines, and therapies. But while the researchers stay firmly focused on the now, they are also looking towards tomorrow. "We must refine our capacity to track the rise of new viral variants," warns Daley. "We must refine our prevention strategies—an armamentarium of treatments—by developing new antiviral drugs, panviral therapies, and polivariant vaccines. And we must anticipate the post-pandemic realities of COVID-19. A major goal of MassCPR 2.0 will be to define the scope of post-COVID-19 syndrome and understand the long-term effects of multiple organ systems. The knowledge will have relevance beyond this pandemic and, indeed, beyond this pathogen."

Beyond MassCPR, other critical global partnerships have emerged over the course of the past year to bring recent scientific advancements on the virus to the masses, not the least of which is the Access to COVID-19 Tools (ACT) Accelerator and its vaccines pillar, COVAX. The ACT Accelerator is a global philanthropic partnership—not a new agency or institution but rather a framework for collaboration launched by the WHO, the European Commission, France, and the Bill & Melinda Gates Foundation in April 2020.

ACT is focused on accelerating the development and production of COVID-19 tests, treatments, and vaccines (via COVAX) and, perhaps most critically, on ensuring that all people, and all countries, can access and afford these miracles of science. While richer countries have been able to roll out vaccines at no cost to residents, lower-income countries are still struggling to determine how to procure and pay for the vaccines in the first place, much less distribute them fairly across their countries. Rough estimates suggest that it would cost around $30 billion to mass-vaccinate the world—a price rich countries may not choose to shoulder. Take for example the United States, whose portion of the cost to help vaccinate the world is $7 billion. That figure is less than 0.5 percent of what was approved as part of the March 2021 economic stimulus package, mere pennies in relative terms but critical to ending the pandemic.

Global fundraising for health is by no means without precedent, but what makes the ACT Accelerator unique is the burden-sharing formula it proposes to generate the funds. Every country is given a recommended range to contribute, which is adjusted based on GDP and the size of the country itself. The goal is to create a fair and equitable framework to respond to this crisis and future emergencies, including other pandemics—a systematic plan to prevent any country from having to choose again between who lives and who dies.

This collective solution to the problem at hand also has scientists in the lead, with researchers monitoring the vaccine landscape and advising COVAX on the most suitable candidates based on scientific merit and scalability and with major pharmaceutical companies committing to providing hundreds of millions of doses—eventually billions—to distribute around the world. Scientists have not only worked together to develop COVID treatments and vaccines, but they are among the loudest voices calling for rich countries to collaborate and to deploy their wealth across all countries to end the disease.

Yet even with these remarkable scientific efforts, there is perhaps no better indicator of the extent to which the scientific community is focused on collaboration than by how entirely the scientific publication process has been upended. Publication in a well-respected journal is a competitive and highly prized honor, considered so by even the most accomplished scientists. Whereas in the past, researchers were willing to wait months and sometimes more than a year for the distinction, those imperatives have since been set aside. Researchers now proactively share preprint versions of their studies immediately after they determine their results, not only for recognition but in the hopes that their discoveries will help other scientists further their own. Between the start of the pandemic in December 2019 and November 2020, around 75,000 scientific papers were published on COVID-19, with one third published as preprints, released to other scientists and the public at large, before being fully reviewed and accepted for journal publication.

As scientists choose to forgo some of the academic recognition that comes with waiting for traditional publication, the journals themselves have shifted their approach as well, rethinking work flows to publish COVID-related papers much faster than normal. Yet this has not been without consequence. In the spring of 2020, two COVID studies were famously retracted over concerns about the veracity of the primary data. Some journals have admitted they may need to slow the process down again to ensure the quality of the work. Still, the knowledge gained has arguably outweighed the risks, given that the rapid advancements on vaccines, treatments, and our understanding of the disease are owed in large part to the immediate and transparent release of new data.

The question still remains whether this sense of shared purpose and transparent cooperation is a temporary measure or the beginning of a new era of scientific collaboration and global partnership. I can't help but hope that this is indeed the beginnings of a new milestone in human achievement. Science is a tradition built on thousands of years of incremental progress. Imagine the exponential increase if our collaborative efforts continued–a global community united against the most pressing economic, social, and environmental problems of our time.

As Daley of the Harvard Medical School and MassCPR put it, "I cannot help but think that [it] provides a blueprint for moonshot projects that bring together the strongest and most dynamic forces of our formidable, biomedical ecosystem. What if we could marshal these forces against future pandemics, other diseases, and larger global challenges? I dare to imagine the possibilities."

With all the tragedy of the past year and the losses we have suffered, this revolution in the scientific community and beyond may be the one exquisite thing to emerge.

This is an opinion and analysis article.

About the Author

William A. Haseltine is a former Harvard Medical School professor and founder of the university's cancer and HIV/AIDS research departments. He also serves as chair and president of the global health think tank ACCESS Health International. He has founded more than a dozen biotechnology companies and is the author, most recently, of Variants! The Shape-Shifting Challenge of COVID-19.

Astronomy Tool Can Now Detect COVID in Breath

By Starre Vartan

Astronomers and physicists have long used a laser-based sensor called an "optical frequency comb" to study the material makeup of the cosmos and to make timekeeping more accurate. But the COVID pandemic has pushed this versatile tool from the world of space and physics into health care.

Optical frequency combs are lasers that simultaneously shoot pulses of light at multiple frequencies. Because these superfast pulses are precisely spaced along the light spectrum—from infrared through the visible colors to ultraviolet—they form a series of peaks on a graph of the frequencies that look like the teeth of a comb. This "comb" can be used in a variety of ways. For instance, different types of molecules absorb different colors of light; by detecting which colors of light are absorbed near specific frequencies, the comb can identify specific molecules in an air sample. In a recent study, scientists proved this tool can detect COVID from Breathalyzer-type tests in which subjects simply blow into a tube—potentially paving the way for fast, noninvasive diagnostic tests for a multitude of diseases.

Every time humans exhale, we expel more than 1,000 kinds of trace molecules called volatile organic compounds, or VOCs. "Changes in VOC profiles can be linked to specific health conditions," says Cristina Davis, associate vice chancellor for interdisciplinary research and strategic initiatives at the University of California, Davis. Scholars have known for millennia that certain breath odors are associated with clinical diseases or disorders. References in ancient Greek and Chinese medical literature indicate that doctors used the nose as a diagnostic tool, Davis says. More recently, dogs have been trained to identify some diseases in humans—and laser comb detectors also need training, says physicist Jun Ye, co-author of the new study. "We are training our frequency comb nose using machine learning, and once it's trained, it becomes an electronic dog—with much greater sensitivity," Ye says.

This powerful artificial nose has the advantage of being able to sniff out disease in a way that's quick and noninvasive, says the study's lead author, Qizhong Liang, a graduate student at the University of Colorado Boulder. For maximum accuracy, Liang adds, positive results from the new technology's COVID tests should be followed up with a more reliable PCR test. But for quick screening at airports, concert venues, or hospitals, it could beat other methods, such as body temperature scans, that are used to assess potential COVID infection without requiring an invasive nose swab.

Frequency combs can do more than identify molecules. They were originally developed in the 1990s to make more accurate optical atomic clocks, for which the inventors won the 2005 Nobel Prize in Physics. The combs can measure the natural oscillation of atoms so precisely that they have become an indispensable component of atomic clocks, which keep time incredibly well by counting these oscillations. In astronomy, researchers use optical frequency combs to measure the frequencies of light coming from distant stars; disruptions can indicate a star has an exoplanet. In atmospheric science, they have been used to study greenhouse gases. And in 2008, Ye and his colleagues at JILA (a joint institute of the National Institute of Standards and Technology and the University of Colorado Boulder) first proved that the technology could be used as a breath test for disease biomarkers. They set this finding aside, but global events suddenly gave them a very good reason to revive the work in April 2020. "Using breath as a diagnostic tool has been around for a while," Davis says, "but I think it took a pandemic for research interest to really to really be moved forward."

Shortly after the COVID pandemic began, Ye got a call from his colleagues at the National Academies of Sciences, Engineering, and Medicine and the Air Force Office of Scientific Research. They wanted to know whether his early frequency comb "Breathalyzer" research might help develop a noninvasive COVID test.

Ye and his team started by updating their 2008 technology. The researchers extended the laser comb's frequency range from the near-infrared region of the spectrum into the mid-infrared part—where molecules absorb light two to three times more strongly. That signal boost allowed the researchers to improve the tool's detection sensitivity by 1,000-fold, letting them identify molecules at extremely low concentrations on the scale of hundreds of parts per trillion.

Next, Ye's team collected breath samples from 170 University of Colorado Boulder students and staff from May 2021 to January 2022. Each participant received conventional PCR nasal swab COVID tests, and about half were positive. The researchers then used the frequency comb to analyze light-absorption patterns among molecules in the participants' breath. Applying machine learning to the frequency comb data, combined with the already-known PCR data on who was positive or negative, they found six "discriminating molecules" that indicated COVID infection. The work was described in a paper published in April in the *Journal of Breath Research*.

Liang says AI was key to the project's success because of the vast amount of information the frequency comb gathers when analyzing breath. "Machine learning can analyze all of this data simultaneously and can automatically figure out the best way of utilizing all of that discriminating information to make a prediction model," he says.

Frequency combs aren't the only way to test human breath for COVID or other diseases. Other methods include gas chromatography/mass spectrometry systems such as the InspectIR test, which received emergency use authorization from the U.S. Food and Drug Administration in April 2022. In such chemistry-based techniques, the gas molecules to be analyzed are separated by an inert gas, broken down into fragments, and then measured. Davis calls these types of tests the "gold standard," but they require time, specialized training and bulky equipment that limits their use to the lab. Davis has been working on a smaller, portable type of test, an ion mobility spectrometer, which identifies substances based on the mobility of their molecules in an electric field. Other options use chemicals that bind to VOCs to isolate and test them. "There are more than 15 companies working on a variety of these kinds of tests," Davis says.

The frequency comb technology is different, Liang says, because it uses laser spectroscopy and therefore "detects the molecules in breath in a nondestructive way." By this he means the comb does not cause a sample to degrade or create any unwanted by-products, as breath tests that rely on chemical reactions can. Frequency comb technology also has the potential to be really, really fast: it could potentially eventually provide results in seconds, compared with minutes in other breath tests.

That said, you probably won't see laser combs the next time you catch a flight. "Breath tests, in general, have not reached prime time yet," says Wilbur Lam, a COVID test expert, pediatrician and biomedical engineer at Emory University and the Georgia Institute of Technology. With the frequency comb method, he says, "you get an optical signal, and whether that optical signal is truly indicative of a COVID infection really has to be proven. Right now, they're showing some correlation. But how does it correlate with other types of conditions that could affect the breath?"

If frequency comb "Breathalyzers" do prove themselves in further research, they could make a huge difference in many clinical settings beyond rapid testing for COVID. Study co-author Kristen Bjorkman, director of interdisciplinary research at the BioFrontiers Institute, suggests this technology might one day be used to detect chronic obstructive pulmonary disease, kidney failure, lung and pancreatic cancers, and even Alzheimer's disease. Multiple early studies have provided preliminary evidence that the contents of exhaled breaths can be used for these diagnoses.

Breathalyzer-style tests could also be ideal for diagnosing children, and Ye says some pediatricians have already approached him about a frequency comb test for asthma in kids. When a child shows up sick at the emergency room, Ye explains, a lot of invasive tests are required to determine if the symptoms are caused by a bacterial or viral illness or asthma. He says one Denver-based pediatrician told him, "'Imagine you can do a breath analysis on children, which is totally noninvasive. Kids won't cry if they have to just donate a breath.'"

About the Author

Starre Vartan is a science writer and investigative reporter at work on a book challenging cultural myths and health misinformation about women's bodies (Hachette, 2024). She began her career as an environmental geologist in New England, wrote screenplays on science subjects for HBO and CBS, ran a successful blog in the mid-aughts, and has been published in National Geographic, New Scientist, Undark, *CNN and more. A graduate of Syracuse University and Columbia University, she is a dual citizen of the U.S. and Australia and splits her time between the Seattle and Sydney areas.*

Zapping the Vagus Nerve Could Relieve Some Long COVID Symptoms

By Shi En Kim

Can a condition as gnarly and disparate as long COVID be treated without drugs? Social media is buzzing over an experimental therapy that taps the vagus nerve, which acts as the body's "information superhighway" by carrying crucial signals between the brain and various internal organs. A mild electrical zap to this long cranial nerve triggers a rush of autonomic responses associated with relaxation—and may confer health benefits well beyond this.

Researchers are increasingly recognizing that long COVID is as much a neurological disorder as a cardiovascular and respiratory one. Treatment studies have highlighted the condition's neurological aspects, including some that are potentially related to the vagus nerve. Early small-scale trials of vagal stimulation have seen reductions in hallmark long COVID symptoms such as chronic fatigue, headaches, and irregular blood pressure. Another study demonstrated that the devices used to send electrical stimulation through the skin are safe and easy to use at home—offering convenience, accessibility, and less risk of contagion. Scientists are still studying which long COVID symptoms this technique can reliably address, which patients will benefit and how long the effects last. In any case, the vagus nerve's influence throughout the body appears to be key for treating some of the all-encompassing manifestations of long COVID.

"Your body is an electrical and chemical organ," says Peter Staats, co-chair of the Vagus Nerve Society and co-founder of the neuromodulation company electroCore. "Modern medicine has been really focused on the chemical side of things. And it's time to be focusing a little bit more on the electrical side."

Vagus nerve stimulation is already used to treat some other thorny neurological conditions. Implantable stimulators were first approved for epilepsy in 1997 and for depression in 2005. But despite the procedure's promise for treating long COVID, researchers say it won't be enough on its own. Long COVID is an unresolved enigma that's tricky to understand, let alone diagnose or treat. Symptoms vary wildly between individuals, and no single approach can address the viral aftermath throughout the body. Experts say combination therapy appears best for lifting people out of this chronic condition. But vagus nerve stimulation could be a niche tool in the long COVID treatment arsenal. It has potential to address neurological symptoms in a way that limited pharmacological solutions so far have not.

"Whenever we have a single treatment option, we're generally pretty wary of saying this is going to be the cure-all," says Stephanie Grach, an internist at the Mayo Clinic. But "at this point, almost any sort of management or treatment option that could feasibly help a number of people is a game changer."

Stress Buster

The vagus nerve—a bundle of fibers that run from the brain stem and fan out around the body—is the impresario of our involuntary background processes and organ functions. It's also part of the parasympathetic nervous system, which is in charge of calming the body after a stressful event. During this recovery phase, the heart rate slows to normal, the immune system lets down its guard, and the digestive system starts up again. The vagus nerve acts as an "off" switch to the sympathetic system's fight-or-flight mode. This nerve is also activated during activities such as yoga, meditation, and slow breathing, all of which commonly leave practitioners feeling calm and restful.

Electrical stimulation harnesses the vagus nerve's healing power on command more easily. Some people may be able to reengage their own dysfunctional vagus nerve through mindfulness exercises, but most need an external aid. That includes many who live with long COVID, given that they often have severe tissue damage and depleted energy levels. "To tell somebody who has struggled with long COVID for three years and has seen 500 doctors to go do some mindfulness–that's not going to go over well," says Mayo Clinic internist Ravindra Ganesh, who is currently leading a clinical trial of vagus nerve stimulation for long COVID using electroCore devices.

During the early days of the pandemic, researchers quickly noticed that several symptoms of acute COVID infection were similar to those of the vagus nerve going haywire. People hospitalized with COVID often suffered from the so-called cytokine storm, in which the infection triggered an excessive, runaway immune response that eventually turned inward to wreck the host's own tissues.

After the initial infection waned, a large percentage of those experiencing long COVID still reported symptoms typically seen with vagal dysfunction. And this past June researchers found smoking-gun evidence: postmortems of deceased people who had COVID revealed viral RNA and inflammation cells in the vagal tissues, indicating the virus had infiltrated and damaged this key nerve.

To many researchers, jump-starting a decommissioned vagus nerve seemed like an obvious solution for treating long COVID. "It's a really fundamental nerve," says Michael VanElzakker, a neuroscientist at Massachusetts General Hospital. Targeting it as a treatment approach "really ought to be considered and deserves more research."

The Long COVID Connection

Researchers think vagus nerve stimulation weakens long COVID symptoms by turning up the body's parasympathetic pathways. One sign of heightened sympathetic activity is when an immune system keeps firing up, even after the initial infection has passed. The vagus nerve quiets this overactive defense by reducing the production of cytokines, signaling chemicals that promote inflammation. In 2000 researchers discovered the vagus nerve's anti-inflammatory role when they found that stimulating it reduced lethal septic shock in rats exposed to bacterial toxins. Many scientists think reactivating the vagus nerve could also potentially reset immunity in people with acute COVID or chronic symptoms.

Rousing the portion of the vagus nerve entering the brain stem might also engage neighboring cortical areas that are involved in memory and attention, according to Elisabetta Burchi, head of translational research at the neuromodulation start-up Parasym. Such stimulation sets off a release of neurotransmitter chemicals, which may help reduce long COVID's neurocognitive effects. The evidence is still inconclusive, though. One preprint study that's awaiting peer review found that vagal stimulation had only a minimal impact on "brain fog," a frequently reported symptom of long COVID.

So far pilot studies have demonstrated that vagus nerve stimulation works best for reducing long COVID's debilitating fatigue. Researchers have been encouraged that some participants in these studies reported improvements–but they have noted that some did not. "There is no trial of any drug or anything I've ever done in all my years that makes a patient so well that he or she no longer fulfills criteria for chronic fatigue syndrome," says Benjamin Natelson, a neurologist at Mount Sinai, who has run several clinical studies on vagus nerve stimulation for various health conditions, some of which used devices from electroCore and Parasym. (Natelson says he did not receive funding for the studies from these companies.)

Because the vagus nerve consists of so many fibers, researchers can't control which individual fiber gets triggered to target any particular organ; multiple parasympathetic pathways get turned on at once during stimulation. This may sound worrying, but researchers agree there aren't many negative side effects from excessive parasympathetic action. If such a device is used properly, the worst potential complications will probably be mild skin irritation from the electrical zaps or diarrhea from an overstimulated digestive system.

Vagal therapy still has scientific gaps to address, so doctors are hesitant to prescribe it broadly for long COVID before a confirmatory trial is complete. Scientists are still working out treatment details, including the best delivery method. For example, electroCore's strategy is a series of mild shocks with a handheld device that a user can touch to either side of the neck for a few minutes every day. Staats, the firm's co-founder, says this is where the vagus bundle is thickest, making it the most effective stimulation site. Other researchers, including those at Parasym, say taming long COVID's symptoms requires a longer stimulation time. These scientists note that the tip of a vagal branch ends in the folds of the ear. Wearing a hands-free, earbudlike clip there could be a relatively convenient way to deliver an hour of electrical stimulation daily.

But electrically stimulating the neck or ear might not activate the entire vagal column, argues Gemma Lladós, an infectious disease physician at the Germans Trias i Pujol University Hospital in Spain. She suggests a more invasive approach: a device implanted under the skin directly over the vagal bundle to deliver close-up and continuous stimulation, similar to implants for epilepsy and depression. Lladós's team is finalizing plans for a 2024 clinical study on treating long COVID with a vagus nerve implant.

Sticker Shock

There's also one glaring caveat to vagus nerve stimulation: the price. The electroCore device, for example, is offered on a pay-per-use basis that can cost a person more than $7,000 per year without any discounts. Parasym's stimulator has a one-time price tag of €699 (approximately $770) and is only sold in Europe (though Natelson says some of the people he treats in the U.S have managed to purchase the device by using European addresses). U.S. regulators have approved electroCore's device and some other companies' versions as well—but exclusively for non-COVID-related problems such as migraines. People with long COVID can buy these products only if their physicians prescribe them off-label, and insurance companies are unlikely to cover the cost without specific approval for long COVID.

Researchers caution against trying to build one's own device or purchasing untested versions on the internet. Vagus nerve stimulation involves running an electrical current close to your heart or brain. "Let's not mess with that," Ganesh says. Approved medical devices are calibrated to be safe, but an unapproved device with incorrect settings could slow or stop the heart. In extreme cases, vagal tampering can lead to sudden death.

As with any long COVID therapy, the key is pacing to ration one's energy levels according to the body's limits, Grach says. At the Mayo Clinic, she often sees patients who are so excited to embark on a new treatment that they push their body too far and eventually crash. "If you continue to push past the reserve that your body has," Grach says, "you're not going to end up feeling the benefit of the interventions regardless."

About the Author

Shi En Kim is a science writer based in Washington, D.C. Her work has appeared in Chemical & Engineering News, National Geographic, Hakai Magazine, Slate, Science News, *and more. Follow her on X (formerly Twitter) @goes_by_kim.*

The Pandemic Set Off a Boom in Diagnostics

By Roxanne Khamsi

A decade ago Willy Ssengooba began crisscrossing Uganda, training health-care workers on how to use a new machine to detect tuberculosis. The deadly lung disease infects around 90,000 people in the East African nation annually, but it can sometimes take months to diagnose using traditional methods such as culturing samples of coughed-up sputum. These new machines used rapid molecular testing to yield results within a couple of hours, meaning patients who tested positive could immediately be referred for lifesaving treatment. Ssengooba, who is scientific director of the mycobacteriology research unit at the Makerere University College of Health Sciences in Kampala, helped to set up 265 of the devices in clinics around the country. By increasing the number of early diagnoses—especially among vulnerable groups such as children and people living with HIV—deaths associated with tuberculosis dropped, too. Ssengooba saw this as a major success and wanted to deploy more machines. But it was hard to make politicians aware of the technology's power.

Then COVID arrived. Not long after the first case was reported in Uganda on March 21, 2020, Ssengooba received a message from a commissioner under the Ministry of Health. It had quickly become apparent that most of the new cases were coming through the border crossings, so screening people there would be a priority. Could Ssengooba make it possible to test everyone who wanted to enter Uganda? His entire country was counting on him.

Ssengooba and his team began facilitating the collection of nasal swabs taken from truckers at popular entry points, where imported goods are brought into the landlocked country. Those samples—sometimes more than 1,000 a day—then needed to be shuttled 150 miles to Kampala. The capital city was the nearest place with laboratory technology set up to run a process known as polymerase chain reaction–or PCR. Using fluorescent probes that latch onto portions of the coronavirus genetic sequence, these massive machines could determine whether a sample was positive for the genetic material of SARS-CoV-2.

Ssengooba's team had to shuttle the samples themselves. A crew of about 50 workers collected the samples in pickup trucks and delivered them to the lab, then turned around to go back for the next batch, spending long, exhausting nights on the road. As the pandemic intensified, they couldn't keep up. Truckers awaiting their test results were stalled at the border for days, in part because the sample analysis in Kampala would sometimes take up to 72 hours to return a result. A queue of trucks formed, stretching for kilometers, holding up the import of everything from home appliances to construction materials to replacement parts for cars. Making matters worse, authorities had closed the airport.

The government was desperate to alleviate the backlog. Ssengooba considered the 265 machines he had set up throughout Uganda over the years to test for tuberculosis. He realized he could repurpose some of those small PCR machines to test for the coronavirus by using a different sample-processing cartridge. He relocated that equipment directly to the border entry points and engineered some basic infrastructure (electrical power; benchtop safety spaces) to support their use. Unlike the lab setup in Kampala, which requires multiple machines spread across different rooms and experienced technicians to prepare and process the samples, these so-called GeneXpert modules were automated and about the size of a printer. They still used PCR technology but could return results on the spot in around half an hour.

By May the first COVID testing systems were working at the crossing point in the Kenya-Uganda border town of Malaba, reducing the waiting time for truck drivers from days to around half an hour. Within a week the equipment was set up at two other major border points. Many countries, even wealthy ones, struggled to get COVID screenings off the ground in the early months of the pandemic. But

Ssengooba understood how to balance the needs of public health and the economy. By cobbling together testing infrastructure where it was most needed, he was preventing disease while keeping critical goods flowing into the country.

Ssengooba's creative repurposing of Uganda's limited testing resources was "tremendous," says Wilber Sabiiti, an expert at the University of St. Andrews in Scotland in the development of diagnostics tests. After Ssengooba had worked tirelessly for years to try to make PCR testing more accessible for tuberculosis, his efforts finally seemed to be getting validated. The pandemic, he says, has clarified the urgency of deploying PCR technology more widely for all kinds of infectious diseases, especially to politicians, who are now allocating more money to the technology. "The SARS-CoV-2 outbreak has been like a blessing in disguise for the scale-up of molecular assays," he says.

Ssengooba is hardly alone in his thinking. Alex Greninger, assistant director of the clinical virology labs at the University of Washington Medical Center, says that in the past, the facility where he works typically ran 50,000 PCR tests a year for diseases such as influenza and HIV. Between early 2020 and the end of 2021, it had done four million PCR tests, mainly for COVID. Unlike in the past, however, the results have been vital to informing immediate behaviors: those who test positive self-isolate or are kept in a special ward of a hospital. This has created a massive new reliance on testing to guide such decisions. "We [did] 81 years' worth of molecular testing in the virology lab in the first 22 months" of the pandemic, Greninger says. He expects the demand for PCR testing to stick around even after COVID ebbs. The general public is much more aware of virology now, he says, and as rapid antigen tests become a more routine part of living amid COVID and its potential future surges, people will seek out PCR tests to confirm positive results.

COVID has not just increased the scale of disease testing and created demand from pretty much everyone; it has also spurred the adoption of more advanced versions of the tests themselves. Hospital systems have begun purchasing PCR machines that are small enough to install at a doctor's office so that samples do not have to be sent offsite to a huge, centralized lab. That means patients can get a diagnosis on the spot and isolate immediately, if needed—and take whatever antiviral or antibiotic is most appropriate. Companies and university researchers around the globe who are working on PCR technologies say there is escalating interest in their innovations, such as handheld versions that would make testing anywhere—from supermarket parking lots to remote villages—more feasible.

All of this may benefit more than just individual patients. As the emergence of the quick-spreading Omicron variant demonstrated in late 2021, ramping up testing at the population level is crucial to keep tabs on how COVID might morph and push hospital systems (among other sectors of society) to a breaking point. The sweeping uptake of PCR for COVID could also pave the way for stronger public health surveillance systems that can spot future pandemics by scanning for dozens of pathogens at once. According to Jeffrey Townsend, a biostatistician at the Yale School of Public Health, PCR is a powerful tool to use for disease surveillance, and "there's a lot of people who say we need to be doing it even more."

A Strange Trip

In 1983 Kary Mullis was driving up to his cabin on the northern coast of California with his girlfriend, a chemist at the biotechnology company where they had been hired to synthesize genetic fragments. Mullis had spent earlier years completing a Ph.D. at the University of California, Berkeley, where he would trip on LSD while making new chemicals. His girlfriend had fallen asleep, and as he drove he had a vision of molecules dancing on the mountain road. It was then that the idea for polymerase chain reaction came to him. He pulled over the car and scribbled down his thoughts. It won him a Nobel Prize a decade later.

At its heart, PCR is a method of making copies of genetic sequences. There are now many dozens of different kinds of PCR, but the most basic form that Mullis devised started with a tiny bit of DNA and then used various cycles of heating and cooling to replicate it. First, the process would heat the DNA to break its double helix structure into two strands. Next, it would cycle to a cooler temperature that would allow specially tailored primers to bind to specific target sequences within the strands. The samples would be warmed up again, and enzymes would get to work building off those primers to finish replicating the complementary DNA sequences. The cycle would then repeat. Ultimately it yielded a lot of copies of the target strands. Special fluorescent tags were later added to the process to flag the presence of those amplified short sequences of interest.

It became possible to use this method to detect the presence or absence of pathogens: if a virus was present in a person's blood sample, for example, the PCR machine would make a lot of copies of its sequence, and the fluorescent tags would shine brightly. If there was no virus, there would be only darkness.

The incorporation of fluorescent tags meant that the PCR machines could also indicate how *much* virus was in a person's system. If the fluorescent light shined more strongly and sooner in the replication cycling, it meant more virus was present. A PCR could not only detect DNA, it could also detect genetic material known as RNA. This opened up a whole new world of diagnostics because many viruses, such as HIV, are RNA-based organisms. As the AIDS pandemic tore through the globe, doctors wanted to know *how much* HIV was circulating in their patients' bodies and whether the antiviral drugs they prescribed were working to keep the levels low. PCR could finally give them an answer.

The machines that did the analyses, though, required lab technicians with highly specialized expertise to prep samples and took half a day or more to return results. That changed after the U.S. Postal Service launched a competition for technology that could quickly screen mail for deadly anthrax spores, which a bioterrorist sent in letters to the offices of U.S. senators and journalists after 9/11. The winner, announced in 2002, was a GeneXpert prototype from Cepheid, a Silicon Valley diagnostics company founded in the late 1990s. The system automated many of the previously laborious sample preparation steps by using cartridges and valves that pull liquids through tiny channels and mix them together. And it returned results in minutes rather than hours. In the decades since, the GeneXpert platform has received approval to test for pathogens such as norovirus, chlamydia, tuberculosis, and SARS-CoV-2.

Cepheid says there are now more than 40,000 GeneXpert machines around the world, up from 23,000 in 2020. (The diagnostics branch of the major biomedical company Roche also has a PCR machine for clinics that is about the size of a coffee machine.) Increasingly, they are found at doctors' offices and at locations such as the border crossings in Uganda—rather than just at centralized labs. In September 2020 Cepheid received FDA authorization for a GeneXpert test that looks simultaneously for influenza A and B, SARS-CoV-2 and a pathogen that is particularly dangerous in young kids called respiratory syncytial virus. The test results, which can come back in about half an hour, help clinicians know what specific antiviral to give if a patient is sick—Tamiflu for influenza, for example, and Paxlovid for COVID. That is all the more crucial during a pandemic when your infection determines your isolation behavior.

Real-Time Warning Systems

It was not until the past decade or so that scientists established global surveillance systems that rapidly tracked outbreaks of viruses. Testing for pathogens fell to individual labs, and molecular diagnostics approaches such as PCR were expensive or unavailable. Furthermore, to do PCR testing for viruses of interest, scientists needed specific probes that would recognize a genetic sequence in the pathogens. But they lacked easy tools to create these probes. The barriers to conducting PCR and the dearth of repositories to upload such data made tracking the ebb and flow of viruses in populations spotty.

In 2012 the California Department of Public Health received several reports of a mysterious poliolike disease striking children.

It manifested as a sudden onset of muscle weakness in the limbs, sometimes also leading to slurred speech and difficulty moving the eyes. The sick children did not have poliovirus, and health authorities ruled out other possible culprits, including West Nile virus, stroke, and botulism. What the children *did* have was an obscure virus called enterovirus D68, or EV-D68, which had first been identified decades ago. It had recently been linked with acute flaccid myelitis. Although some children make a full recovery from this condition, it can cause permanent paralysis and even death.

Around the same time that acute flaccid myelitis became associated with EV-D68, BioFire Diagnostics, a Utah-based molecular biology company that is now a subsidiary of the global diagnostics giant bioMérieux, began offering a comprehensive PCR-based respiratory test. It looked for 17 viruses and three bacteria in a single deep nasal swab taken from a patient.

Although the respiratory panel does not test specifically for EV-D68, it tests for the presence of the general family of viruses to which it belongs. BioFire wanted to find a way to catch EV-D68 outbreaks so that doctors and public health officials could know to keep patients from infecting others. Along with its academic partners, the company developed and tested an algorithm that was trained on past data to predict hotspots of EV-D68. The real proof of the approach came in 2018, when the algorithm alerted researchers to the emergence of EV-D68 that summer. Nationwide Children's Hospital in Columbus, Ohio, was one of the first places the algorithm identified with a possible uptick in cases of the virus; the team there confirmed the algorithm was right. As a result, the hospital implemented EV-D68 testing to catch cases early and prevent it from spreading.

A related surveillance platform that uses BioFire's PCR test collates data from different sites across the U.S. and other countries around the world on respiratory viruses such as influenza, rhinovirus, and now coronavirus, as well as more than a dozen gastrointestinal pathogens. Unlike the cumbersome data-collection protocols of the past, surveillance systems that continuously collect data directly from connected PCR machines have the potential to be used to detect outbreaks, including those of foodborne disease.

In many ways, this approach—combination PCR tests that cast a wider net to look for more possible pathogens in a given sample—signals the future of PCR. "Their instruments are phoning home, which is totally cool," Greninger says of the BioFire disease-tracking platform, explaining that the broad net it casts could help show where unexpected outbreaks are occurring. The COVID pandemic has made it clear that testing people for viruses even if they are asymptomatic can help identify those who would not otherwise know they are infected, prompting them to isolate before they pass the pathogen unknowingly to others in their community.

Viral evolution can sometimes create a challenge for PCR. Because the primers and probes used in the tests are tailored to look for specific, telltale sequences within a virus, sometimes a new viral variant can evade detection because its sequence has evolved beyond what the test is looking for. Test developers have to constantly ensure the primers and probes are up-to-date. "You need to have a very good understanding of emerging genomes in populations throughout the globe if you're going to have a globally applicable and accurate diagnostic PCR-based test," explains Alexandra Valsamakis, head of clinical development and medical affairs at Roche Diagnostics Solutions.

Yet once scientists have identified new viral variants, they can use PCR testing to track the spread of those variants. This is a capability that the antigen-based testing methods—which look for proteins unique to a particular pathogen—cannot do. The emergence of the Omicron variant has shown how vital it is to track variants. The data pouring in from PCR tests revealed that Omicron was spreading like wildfire compared with the Delta variant that preceded it. As a result, some governments began updating their guidelines and pushing for more booster shots, and some people took the data as a cue to reconsider their social interactions and upgrade the efficacy of their masks.

Some experts worry that even if PCR testing capacity expands to make more of this kind of surveillance possible, it will be hampered by insurance companies that might be unwilling to pay for asymptomatic testing or that hesitate to reimburse tests for pathogens for which no drugs or treatment are yet available. In most cases, insurance companies "pay for vaccines and diagnostics based on individual benefit," says Dan Wattendorf, the Innovative Technology Solutions team director at the Bill & Melinda Gates Foundation. "But we don't really have payment schemes or reimbursement and coverage to find transmission in the community." The problem with coverage for PCR testing has already been a sticking point in the coronavirus pandemic. The U.S. government set up requirements for health insurers to cover PCR testing for COVID, but consumers both with and without coverage have still been left with surprise bills in the thousands of dollars. Whereas PCR technology itself is undoubtedly powerful for disease surveillance, the question of who will foot the bill remains largely unanswered.

How COVID is Shaping the Future of Diagnostics

As COVID created demand for more PCR testing everywhere, it also exposed how most of the technology relies on costly enzymes and single-use plastic parts for sample processing. After successfully setting up the fast-turnaround GeneXpert machines on Uganda's border in the spring of 2020, Ssengooba soon ran out of the cartridges and reagents the machines rely on. In those early months of the pandemic, Uganda requested 500,000 such cartridges from Cepheid, but Ssengooba says the company sent only 30,000. The test maker, he recalls, said that it was barred from sending more cartridges out of the U.S. "We spent the rest of 2020 without access to additional cartridges," Ssengooba says.

Modern PCR machines use plastic trays that traditionally have each contained 96 or 384 small wells to hold samples. To circumvent the need for expensive plastic "consumables" such as tubes and caps, U.K.-based company LGC replaces the tray with a long, flexible polymer tape. Only 0.3 millimeter thick, it can stretch up to 40 meters and has room for 106,368 reaction wells. "That allows you to do 100,000 to 150,000 tests per machine per day, which is 10 times more than any machine in the world at 10 times less cost," Wattendorf says, adding that the Gates foundation has partnered with LGC and Northwell Health, the largest health system in New York State, to try the tape-based method for COVID testing.

Another bottleneck with PCR is that "you have to get the sample very, very purified" before running the test, says biomedical engineer Nicholas Adams. PCR machines are calibrated to run reactions at specific temperatures, and impurities such as salts and proteins from patient samples and added preservatives can throw that off. Removing impurities is tough. To avoid that step, Adams and Frederick Haselton, both at Vanderbilt University, had the idea of adding DNA that is a mirror version of the target genetic sequence the PCR test is trying to detect. These mirror sequences are "left-handed"—meaning that they twist in the opposite direction of naturally occurring DNA, which is right-handed—so they do not interfere with the detection process. By adding a specific amount of the left-handed DNA and tracking how much of it is copied, Adams can use it as a benchmark to calibrate and confirm that the PCR machine is running without worrying about many impurities. Adams says that by reducing the need for purification with the left-handed DNA—which costs about 11 cents per test—labs could save significant labor and material costs.

Now that COVID has shown how important it is for testing to be accessible, there is more enthusiasm for portable PCR devices. Avleo Technologies has designed a handheld molecular testing machine that gives results in 30 minutes. Another device, from Visby Medical, was initially developed to look for sexually transmitted infections such as chlamydia and gonorrhea (and received FDA clearance for those applications) and has since added testing for SARS-CoV-2. Anavasi Diagnostics' AscencioDx platform, originally developed to detect HIV and flu before the pandemic hit, is being used in trials as a rapid molecular COVID test. In November 2021 the National Institutes of Health awarded $14.9 million to Anavasi to support that initiative.

Diagnostics developers are continuing to tinker with PCR. German engineering company Solarkiosk Solutions is developing a version that runs on solar power, which it is piloting for COVID testing in a remote part of Sumatra where many residents lack access to electricity and diagnostics. Academic labs and start-ups such as Mammoth Biosciences in San Francisco are combining traditional PCR methods with CRISPR gene-editing technology to make the tests more efficient at detecting specific pathogen genes.

At Uganda's border crossings, Ssengooba says that testing, at this moment, anyway, is "very smooth." But nearly 40 years after the idea of PCR was born, the technology is evolving rapidly as a result of the pandemic, and Ssengooba is dreaming big. He is eager to try the handheld disease diagnostics because traditional PCR—including the printer-size machines at the border—still require hookups to the electricity grid and various sample-processing rooms. A portable version, akin to the one in development by Indian company Molbio, could bypass some of these requirements and open up fast-testing access to remote areas for the first time. "This is something that is incredible," he says.

Public health has always been stymied by the hours or days between collecting a sample and delivering the results to the patient; in the meantime, an infected person has left the clinic and gone back to the routines of their life, unwittingly exposing others and delaying treatments that are often more effective if started earlier. COVID, and the stunning transmissibility of Omicron in particular, has laid bare the consequences of that gap—for individual health, community transmission, overburdened hospitals, labor shortages, and so much more. Ssengooba is hopeful that the urgency for closing that gap will persist. When imagining a future where portable PCR tests with on-site results are commonplace, "all of these challenges," he says, "are going to be left behind."

About the Author

Roxanne Khamsi is a science journalist and radio contributor based in Montreal. She has reported extensively on the COVID pandemic.

Pathogen-Sensing Mask Could Detect COVID Infection

By Simon Makin

Masks and testing have been key to the COVID-19 pandemic response—and now devices that combine the two may be on the way. Harvard University and Massachusetts Institute of Technology researchers used synthetic biology to create a face mask that accurately detects the COVID-causing virus.

Synthetic biologists use biological parts to build various devices, including sensors that detect genetic sequences. Previous efforts have used engineered bacteria in these sensors, but living cells bring challenges (like keeping them fed) and biohazard risks. The new research makes wearable devices with freeze-dried "cell-free" circuits built from genes, enzymes, and other cell components, which can be placed on porous, flexible materials and easily stored. (The researchers described adding such circuits to paper in 2014.) "This work's important advance is converting bench-top technology to wearable devices," says bioengineer Xinyue Liu, who develops living sensors at M.I.T. and was not part of the new study. Such tools could allow for simplified on-site testing.

The study, published in *Nature Biotechnology*, describes adding cell-free sensors to elastics, textile threads and paper to detect the virus that causes COVID-19 (SARS-CoV-2), Ebola virus, MRSA, a chemical nerve agent, and more. Some of these sensors, including those used in the new face mask that flags SARS-CoV-2, rely on CRISPR technology: When "guide" RNAs match target DNA, they activate an enzyme that cuts the nucleic acids (the DNA "letters"). This particular enzyme also cuts other nearby nucleic acids, freeing a fluorescent protein that emits light. The technique makes for versatile, "programmable" sensors that could be quickly adapted to detect virus variants.

The prototype mask activates with a push-button that rehydrates the sensor, starting reactions that break the virus apart and amplify its DNA for detection. The full process produces a color change within 90 minutes of activation—say, when worn by a hospital patient. "Breath is a nice source of noninvasive sampling that has the right concentrations," says University of Freiburg sensor expert Can Dincer, who was not involved in the new study. "The application really fits the needs of our current situation."

Sensitivity was similar to most lab tests'. "The 'gold standard' would still be your lab-based PCR tests, but we're in the ballpark," says bioengineer and senior author James Collins. The single-use masks need no power source nor operator expertise and work at typical room temperature and humidity.

Collins hopes to commercialize the mask to sell for around $5. Similar genetic-circuit wearables, he adds, could aid health-care workers, military personnel, first responders, and others in the field.

About the Author

Simon Makin is a freelance science journalist based in the U.K. His work has appeared in New Scientist, *the* Economist, Scientific American *and* Nature, *among others. He covers the life sciences and specializes in neuroscience, psychology and mental health. Follow Makin on X (formerly Twitter) @SimonMakin.*

An Experimental Treatment Could Help COVID Smell Distortion

By Hannah Docter-Loeb

Smell loss, or anosmia, is a well-known symptom of COVID. Some people don't experience full-blown loss but rather changes in or distortion of smell, a condition known as parosmia. Studies estimate that between 25 and 75 percent of those with a COVID infection experience long-term parosmia. Now an injection that blocks nerve pain could potentially provide relief for some people.

The technique, known as a stellate ganglion block, has been used for decades to treat all sorts of pain conditions. During the procedure, specialists inject a local anesthetic into a collection of nerves in the neck to block their activity and thereby reduce pain. Sometimes people receive two injections, which are administered a few days apart on each side of the neck. Now some individuals with long-COVID-induced parosmia are electing to have the procedure, and many of them have reported benefits in early studies. But the procedure remains somewhat unproven, experts say.

Parosmia can be detrimental to a person's well-being. For many with the condition, food has very weird smells and tastes. Cheryl Lezak, a 52-year-old who developed parosmia after a COVID infection in December 2021, describes food as smelling like burned metal and tasting of phlegm.

"It's like being in hell," she says, noting that she ended up using nose plugs in order to eat certain foods. "It's just devastating, and it interrupts your life so much. You don't realize how important [the smell of] food has become or was. You take that for granted."

In addition to being disruptive to day-to-day function, COVID-induced parosmia is linked to anxiety, depression, and suicidal thoughts.

Prior to the pandemic, some research investigated using stellate ganglion blocks for smell-related disorders. As the prevalence of these conditions has increased with COVID, the body of research has grown. Researchers at Jefferson Health in Philadelphia presented some of the most recent findings on the treatment's effectiveness in late November at a Radiological Society of North America conference. In a sample of 54 people, 86 percent of those who reported some improvement after the first injection also reported additional improvement after a second injection. None of the participants reported complications or adverse events. The findings have not yet been published in a scientific journal.

"More than 60 percent of people who have parosmia symptoms after COVID have experienced at least 50 percent relief from the symptoms after one injection," says Adam Zoga, the study's lead author and a professor of musculoskeletal radiology at Jefferson Health. "Most patients are getting significant improvement."

Zoga's team is not the only group of researchers working to evaluate whether stellate ganglion block works for smell distortion caused by COVID. There have been other case studies and surveys that have suggested the treatment's effectiveness. Some pain specialists have carved out a niche for themselves by offering the procedure to treat COVID-related parosmia and potentially other lingering symptoms. In Bryan, Tex., the clinic Republic Pain Specialists administers about 25 stellate ganglion blocks a day, and one of its specialists, David Gaskin, has also published research on the treatment's high success rate.

Personal anecdotes reflect a mix of experiences. Lezak says that although she had a small improvement after the first injection, the second one did nothing. But James Naylor, a 37-year-old in the U.K., who has had parosmia since a probable COVID infection in early 2023, got the block in early October and has seen his smell improve in the past couple of months. "For me, it wasn't the case [that] it got cleared up instantly," he says. "I've been recovering gradually since." Naylor notes that he never tested positive for COVID, though.

The procedure is reasonably safe if it is performed by an experienced specialist, although it is not without risks. Accidentally injecting the block into an artery can be fatal. This risk can be greatly reduced with the help of imaging. But there are still some unknowns.

"We don't know how long the effects are going to last," Zoga says. "The first patient [from the Jefferson Health cohort] is 20 months out, and she has had no recurrence of symptoms." Others who had a positive response to the treatment have not had recurring symptoms either. "But to date I can't say that three years after the injection, the symptoms won't come back," he says.

The mechanism for how the treatment works is unclear. "No one could explain to me how it could possibly work," says Nyssa Farrell, an assistant professor of otolaryngology at Washington University in St. Louis. "But the one thing that was consistent [was that] we were hearing patients say, 'We tried it, and for the first time in months, I could smell and taste normally.'"

Zoga thinks the mechanism might have to do with the way SARS-CoV-2, the virus that causes COVID, infects the body. A growing body of evidence suggests the virus causes inflammation of the nerves that leads to post-COVID symptoms, and the block may be reducing that inflammation. Farrell also highlights that parosmia likely involves a central nervous system processing change in which the nerves remain functional, indicated by the fact that people with parosmia can detect odors, but the inflammation causes a "miswiring" so that smell signals are distorted when they come to the brain.

Many insurance companies are hesitant to reimburse people for the procedure, however. While Zoga says he was able to get his patients' insurance to cover the stellate ganglion block by listing it as a peripheral nerve injection, Gaskin's patients primarily pay out of pocket. Gaskin charges $500 for each injection, so if one of his patients opts to receive it on both sides of their neck, they will looking at a bill of $1,000 for the procedure alone. Naylor says he paid £2,500 (about $3,000) for his two injections.

Randomized controlled trials—which are considered the gold standard for medical research because they compare a control group with a treatment group—are important to fully assess the procedure and convince insurance companies that it is worth reimbursement.

Farrell and her team are currently recruiting for one such study in which people who have had parosmia for at least six months and report it as "bothersome" will receive either a stellate ganglion block or a placebo injection and be evaluated for improvement.

"If it's not controlled, you just don't know," Farrell says. "There's always a placebo effect, and you don't want to negate that placebo effect—it's a great effect to have. But at the same time, if it's just placebo that's causing these changes, do you really want to take the risk of putting a needle in your neck?"

About the Author

Hannah Docter-Loeb is a freelance writer based in Washington, D.C.

Section 4: Lockdown Legacy

COVID Changed the World of Work Forever

By Christina Maslach & Michael P. Leiter

Hardly anyone has made it through the pandemic with their work life unchanged. Millions of people have lost jobs, been placed on furlough, or switched to working from home. Essential workers have continued in place but often with major changes to their workloads, including additional safety procedures and an awareness of infectious disease as a new workplace hazard. According to the Bureau of Labor Statistics, employment dropped by 20.5 million people in the U.S. alone in April 2020. Service providers were hit most intensely: 7.7 million jobs were lost in the leisure and hospitality sector, with 5.5 million of them in food service or drinking establishments.

The shift to remote work led to the complete collapse of the work-home boundary, especially for parents juggling child care and homeschooling with job demands. Poorly timed or endless Zoom meetings interfered with people's ability to get work done and sometimes harmed relationships with colleagues. Essential workers often discovered that their employers' only strategy to bridge the gap created by increased demand was for them to work harder—reinforcements were not on the way. Many employees had to deal with inadequate personal protective equipment while feeling unfairly treated. And it became more difficult for everyone to relax and recover from their ongoing exhaustion as entertainment and fitness facilities closed. Because of these changes, workers experienced more stressful exhaustion, became more negative and cynical about the workplace and felt an erosion of self-confidence—the triple markers of burnout.

At the same time, other people—especially those with comfortable home offices and few parental responsibilities—found benefits in working remotely. Being on their own gave them greater control with fewer distractions. The absence of commuting gave people more time and energy while saving them money. People who had been working in unpleasant or hostile workplaces were now free from disrespectful encounters.

The pandemic has taught many people that the job does not have to be the way it was. This realization may be one reason that many are not going back to their old jobs. At the end of 2021, the service provider and hospitality sectors were facing major challenges in enticing people back to these low-paid, heavy-demand jobs, with many positions remaining empty. At the same time, 4.5 million Americans (3 percent of the workforce) voluntarily quit their jobs in November, reflecting both discontent with their current positions and the desire to find better ones. But solving the burnout problem cannot fall to individual workers. The workplace must change. People burn out because their employers have not successfully managed chronic job stressors. We must place a stronger focus on modifying or redesigning workplace conditions. How can job environments be places that help people thrive rather than wearing them down?

People whose work lives got better over the past two years can generally thank personal resources–a comfortable room of one's own–rather than foresight from their employers. But employers can learn a lot from attending to what helped people be more productive and satisfied during this time. For example, workers were less distracted by pointless meetings and open office settings and were able to focus on meaningful tasks rather than being burdened by busywork. Some companies are trying to entice workers with higher pay or time off. Improving job conditions has even more potential for enduring impact.

Work takes up a lot of people's time, talent, and potential–and workers are increasingly demanding that it offer a sustainable and rewarding quality of life in return.

About the Authors

Christina Maslach is a professor of psychology at the University of California, Berkeley.

Michael P. Leiter is a former professor of psychology at Acadia University and St. Mary's University, both in Nova Scotia. He also runs a private consulting company.

The Pandemic Showed the Promise of Cities with Fewer Cars

By Andrea Thompson

During COVID's first wave, the streets of New York and other major cities became eerily empty. Mournful sirens replaced the usual bustle and din. But urban dwellers also heard something new: an abundance of birdsong. During walks outside—the only safe respite beyond their apartments—they breathed cleaner air. Lockdowns had meant fewer cars on the roads, and the effects were unmissable. Levels of nitrogen dioxide—a by-product of fossil fuels burned in cars and in electricity generation—were 30 percent lower along the I-95 corridor from Washington, D.C., to Boston in March 2020 compared with previous years. Come summer, people sat at outdoor extensions of restaurants built in parking zones and moved around on newly added bike lanes. These incidental adaptations to the pandemic allowed residents to *experience* the benefits of shifting away from the "car is king" status quo in a way that policy proposals for climate-friendly infrastructure never could, explains Christian Brand, an environmental scientist with the Transport Studies Unit at the University of Oxford. Now, he says, "they know what's possible."

Some fought to keep it that way. Paris has been a leader of this sustainability shift nudged along by the pandemic. The French capital already had plans to tamp down car use and encourage cycling before COVID emerged, but in late spring 2020 some 50 kilometers of pop-up bike lanes, called *coronapistes*, were added literally overnight. They are now a permanent part of Paris's cycling network, with more in the works.

These strides, Brand says, came in no small part because of political will. Paris Mayor Anne Hidalgo made climate change a focus of her reelection campaign. Besides providing subsidies for purchasing and repairing bicycles, she emphasized the health benefits of reducing car emissions, calling pollutants and a contagious respiratory virus "a dangerous cocktail." In other cities, like New York, changes were more modest or temporary. Shutdowns may have revealed the possibility of safer, healthier streets—but it was often a fleeting vision.

About the Author

Andrea Thompson is an associate editor covering the environment, energy and earth sciences. She has been covering these issues for 16 years. Prior to joining Scientific American, *she was a senior writer covering climate science at* Climate Central *and a reporter and editor at* Live Science, *where she primarily covered earth science and the environment. She has moderated panels, including as part of the United Nations Sustainable Development Media Zone, and appeared in radio and television interviews on major networks. She holds a graduate degree in science, health and environmental reporting from New York University, as well as a B.S. and an M.S. in atmospheric chemistry from the Georgia Institute of Technology.*

We Indulged Our Child During COVID Lockdown. Did That Change Him?

By Michael Venutolo-Mantovani

There was a time when my wife Emily and I spoiled the heck out of our son.

He was our first child and just two years old when COVID restrictions sent nearly everyone into lockdown. Because we were trying to have another, and Emily's elderly father lived under our care, we spent most of the first half of my son's second year alone at home.

We did our best to keep him sated with games and his few buckets of toys. We relied heavily on screen time to keep him occupied while Emily and I did our best to keep our careers afloat. We took countless walks in the woods behind our house, playing in the knee-high water of the small, clear creek that runs past our neighborhood.

As COVID measures started to lift, daycares and kids' museums in our town were still closed, and playdates ever tricky, as coordinating and maintaining everyone's level of comfort was a feat unto itself.

Considering everything he had endured and his general state of isolation, Emily and I bought our son a little gift nearly every time we left the house, figuring it was one of the few ways we could keep him happy, engaged, and entertained in such an unprecedented time.

It was never anything more than tossing a $1 Hot Wheels car into a shopping cart already piled with at-home COVID tests and N95 masks at the local pharmacy. After all, there are only so many hours of *Frozen* a little boy can watch each day (roughly five, empirically speaking). This went on through the end of summer, until he was able to start daycare. Though we slowly weaned the process down from *every time* we left the house to once a week or so, Emily and I suspected we might be doing some lasting harm to our son, creating a little boy who expected gifts every time one of us left the house.

As time went on—and with the help of the amazing caregivers at his daycare program—Emily and I began to untangle this idea. Yet, four years later, Emily and I occasionally see remnants of that "spoiled" little boy, often manifested in selfishness. Though those moments are growing fewer and further between, owing much to his experience of becoming a big brother, our son will still pout or occasionally have an outright meltdown when met with a firm "no," especially if a new toy is involved. He's quicker to recover now that he's getting a bit older. But are these tantrums perfectly normal, or are they because Emily and I spoiled him during the lockdown era?

As he is our firstborn, everything our son does is new to us—we don't really know what normal is. Is our son forever changed because of the pandemic lockdown or is he now just an average six-year-old; a kid who is figuring out the world around him while displaying some very standard selfishness?

While much of the research on COVID-related isolation is ongoing, in general, isolation isn't good for children. Social isolation in childhood—when kids are excluded or report feeling lonely—can lead to depression, problems in school, a bleaker outlook on careers, increased body weight, and even heart disease.

But as we are now a couple of years out from the lockdown part of the pandemic, some trends are starting to emerge. A study conducted by Columbia University researchers and their colleagues found that babies born at the beginning of the pandemic had slightly poorer social and motor skills at age six months than babies born just before the pandemic.

Another study published in *JAMA Pediatrics* last year found that children who were exposed to the pandemic between the ages of one and five were "4.39 months behind in development" at age five "compared with those not exposed to the pandemic." And yet another study, also published last year in *JAMA*, found that young children exposed to the pandemic were more likely to experience socioemotional delays compared to children in the pre-pandemic era.

As I read through this research, elements like "increased emotional symptoms and self-regulation difficulties" shot out at me. Was my son experiencing such an increase? Did he have issues self-regulating? Or was he, again, progressing as normal? It's impossible not to wonder. And though the generation of young kids who spent a few months in isolation is hardly an apples-to-apples comparison to children who have had severe and protracted bouts of isolation, it's hard to keep my parenting brain from straying to the worst-case scenario. After all, it's often what the parenting brain is programmed to do.

I'm heartened by the fact that my son is beginning to show greater signs of selflessness. He's always been quick to share his toys, but now my wife and I are noticing how much more readily he accepts no for an answer. I'm also curious to know how much of that has to do with the normal development of a child, as studies have shown it's around age six that kids begin to shed some of their childhood self-centeredness, to develop more empathy for people and the world around them. It's at this age, my son's age, that children's executive function skills mature, which allows them to better manage their own distress and recognize the feelings and needs of those around them. And so, according to that metric, our little boy is right on schedule. Still, even if he is progressing emotionally, I have to assume that six months of lockdown has left some kind of an imprint on him.

Almost 15 million children were born in America between 2017 and 2020, and 90 percent of brain development occurs before kindergarten. The idea that the world might have a microgeneration of lockdown babies is hardly a stretch. It's not clear how that will manifest. Ongoing research will hopefully answer these questions once and for all.

But, knowing what we know, I think we can remain hopeful—kids who were in isolation for six months won't have the same outcomes as children who have been isolated longer or more frequently. Considering as much, the best we can do is hope ongoing research shows that the long-term effects of the pandemic isolation were minimal.

During lockdown, everyone had struggles. For people like me and Emily, parents of young children, it was juggling jobs and new parenthood while trying to keep our baby happy, occupied, and developmentally safe and sound. In the end, we did what we had to do to make it to the end of the day in one piece. We indulged our son, knowing full well it might have long-term effects. Now, as we move forward through his life, we are trying to be attuned to his development, to support him and help him thrive in any situation, and, of course, to help him get more comfortable with being told "no."

This is an opinion and analysis article, and the views expressed by the author or authors are not necessarily those of Scientific American.

About the Author

Michael Venutolo-Mantovani is a freelance writer based in Chapel Hill, North Carolina. His work has appeared in the New York Times, National Geographic, GQ, WIRED, The Guardian, *and* The New Republic, *among others.*

Global Emissions Rebound to Pre-COVID Levels

By Rob Jackson, Pierre Friedlingstein, Corinne Le Quéré, Robbie Andrew, Pep Canadell, Glen Peters, & Sam Abernathy

When COVID-19 disrupted the world's economies last year, global carbon dioxide (CO_2) emissions from fossil fuel use fell by 2 billion metric tons. As some of the lead scientists of the Global Carbon Project (an international group that tracks greenhouse gas emissions), we wrote about how to keep this emissions drop going, including how COVID presented opportunities to rethink transportation and why stimulus funds should be used to promote green rather than brown (fossil) energy use.

We also wrote: "Such emissions declines are enormous and unprecedented–but won't last." A car or airplane (or steel plant, for that matter) parked for a year will pollute just as much when it finally returns to service, and it takes years to replace fossil infrastructure with cleaner technologies.

We expected fossil carbon emissions to approach pre-COVID levels when global economic activity returned closer to normal. And now, as we present in papers available online in Earth System Science Data and arXiv.org, they have.

Our new reports suggest that by the end of 2021, global fossil carbon emissions will reach 36.4 billion metric tons of CO_2, a rise of approximately 4.9 percent compared to 2020. This rebound not only cancels out the COVID-19-associated decrease of 5.4 percent we reported in 2020, but almost returns us to 2019 levels, when the world emitted 36.7 billion tons of CO_2.

The rebound is troubling for several reasons. Some people hoped that the record drop in emissions last year would mark the beginning of the sustained decline in carbon emissions needed to keep global average temperature increases below 1.5 or 2 degrees Celsius. That doesn't appear to be the case, at least yet, and won't happen until more fossil fuel infrastructure is replaced by low-carbon technologies.

Because CO_2 stays in the atmosphere for centuries, we need to lower fossil fuel–based carbon emissions to zero—or even remove carbon from the atmosphere—to keep temperatures from rising further. Another 36 billion tons of fossil carbon pollution this year (and any future year) is incompatible with a safe, stable climate. Climate scientists often say, "We're running out of time," but it's true. If the goal is to limit global warming to 1.5 degrees C, we now have at most a decade's worth of CO_2 we can release into the atmosphere, based on current emissions. If we don't meet that goal, we have perhaps 30 years' worth of current emissions before the planet warms 2 degrees C.

Of all fossil fuels, coal and natural gas use contributed the most to this year's emissions rebound, mainly in the industrial and power sectors. Coal use in 2021 is expected to rise above 2019 levels to 15 billion tons of CO_2. Emissions from coal are now only slightly (less than 1 percent) below their 2013 peak. CO_2 emissions from natural gas use in 2021 should also rebound above 2019 levels. Only CO_2 emissions from oil will remain well below 2019 levels this year at about 11.5 billion tons of CO_2.

The resurgence in emissions is global in scope but varies by country and economic sector. Based on data year-to-date, we expect fossil carbon emissions in Europe (EU27) and the United States to rebound by 8 percent in 2021 after declining more than 10 percent in 2020. Transport- and power-based emissions in the United States are still below 2019 levels, but industrial emissions have grown slightly. Europe's transport and industrial emissions have also fully recovered, but its power sector remains well below 2019 levels. India's fossil carbon emissions will jump almost 13 percent this year, just above 2019 levels, attributable to increases in its power sector that outweigh combined decreases that linger in its industrial and transport sectors.

China saw an even larger rebound in its emissions this year. Its estimated fossil emissions in 2021 are 11.2 billion tons of CO_2, an increase of about 4 percent compared with 2020 emissions and 6 percent higher than in 2019. China's post-COVID-19 economic recovery started earlier than in most other countries, and its emissions rebound began earlier, too. Its power and industrial sectors have rebounded the fastest. Coal use has jumped substantially this year in China; its COVID-19 recovery efforts appear to have stimulated activity in industries dependent on coal-fired power.

Some sectors will continue to see suppressed emissions globally, although those declines are largely offset by increased use in other parts of the global economy.

One sector of the global economy that remains strongly affected by COVID-19 is aviation. The International Civil Aviation Organization's latest report released in October predicts that the number of airline passengers will remain 50 percent below 2019 levels this year. Aviation comprises only a few percent of global fossil carbon emissions, though, so even a decline by half this year is relatively modest in terms of absolute emissions ("only" half a billion tons of avoided carbon emissions).

There was at least some good news in the emissions data of 2020 and 2021. Renewables saw strong growth of 10 percent globally in 2020, despite declines in both global energy use and the use of all three fossil fuels (2 percent, 4 percent and 10 percent declines in 2020 for gas, coal, and petroleum, respectively). Moreover, almost two dozen countries that contribute about a quarter of global fossil carbon emissions saw their emissions decline significantly in the decade of 2010–2019 prior to COVID-19. This list of countries includes the United States, Mexico, and Japan, as well as various nations in Europe, including the United Kingdom, France, Germany, and Sweden. In general, we expect fossil carbon emissions to continue declining in these countries in the future.

What will happen in 2022? We can't rule out a further rise in emissions, particularly if transportation returns to prepandemic levels and coal use remains near 2021 levels or, worse, rises further. The ultimate effect of COVID-19 on fossil carbon emissions remains uncertain and will depend on short-term economic incentives and climate policies. Fully one third of the $15–20 trillion in global economic stimulus packages already passed globally is going to fossil fuels and carbon-intensive heavy industries. Here in the U.S., unless the Build Back Better bill passes, very little of our stimulus spending will go to green energy and clean tech. As a result of stimulating fossil-based industries, carbon emissions are likely to continue rising.

COVID-19 demonstrated the scale of emissions reductions that are required, year after year, for climate stabilization. It also showed how much cleaner our air could be in a fossil-free world. Policy makers need to redouble efforts to shape emissions reductions more equitably in the future, without the economic disruption felt mostly by the global poor.

Like millions of people around the world, we're watching the Glasgow climate change conference carefully. Pledges to end deforestation could reduce five or more billion tons of carbon dioxide pollution a year, while preserving global biodiversity. Additionally, at Glasgow, more than 40 countries have pledged to phase out coal use. Notable countries missing from the list include China, India, Australia, and the United States.

About the Authors

All authors are members of the Global Carbon Project, an international group of scientists tracking emissions of CO_2 and other greenhouse gases from land, oceans, industry and agriculture.

Rob Jackson is an Earth scientist at Stanford University.

Pierre Friedlingstein is a climate scientist at the University of Exeter.

Corinne Le Quéré is a climate scientist at the University of East Anglia.

Robbie Andrew is a climate economist at CICERO Norway.

Pep Canadell is a research scientist at CSIRO Oceans and Atmosphere in Australia.

Glen Peters is an energy expert at CICERO Norway.

Sam Abernathy is a Ph.D. student in Applied Physics and Earth System Science at Stanford University.

How Wild Animals Actually Responded to Our COVID Lockdowns

By Douglas Main

When the COVID pandemic hit British Columbia in spring 2020, Golden Ears Provincial Park closed its doors to visitors. No longer could hikers explore its hemlock forests or canoe in its lakes, but at least some of the park's wildlife seemed to appreciate the situation.

During the closure, a camera trap network run by University of British Columbia researchers recorded a significant uptick in mountain lions. In a common, often half-joking cliché of the time, it seemed to many people that nature was "healing."

"It's a romantic idea," says Cole Burton, a conservation biologist and wildlife ecologist at the University of British Columbia and co-author of the study. But, he adds, it's ultimately flawed. The reality is likely much more complicated: While humans were indoors, he notes, the cameras spotted fewer deer. When lockdowns ended and visitors returned, mountain lion recordings dipped again, and deer recordings picked up. But at the Canadian province's more remote Pacific Rim National Park Reserve, a network of camera traps found that black-tailed deer abundance *declined* when people streamed back in.

Such are the contradictory-seeming results Burton and his colleagues found themselves sorting through as they used the pandemic's unique circumstances to try teasing apart some complexities of wildlife responses to humans. Localized results such as the ones above are vital in order to "help us learn more about what the animals are doing and whether we are disturbing them, even when we don't see them," he says, "and that is important to me both personally and professionally." In trying to make sense of such contrasting findings, Burton wondered what patterns might emerge from gathering relevant data from all around the world.

He put out an invitation to collaborate and eventually teamed up with hundreds of researchers worldwide, amassing data from 102 survey sites in 21 countries. This included observations from 5,400 camera traps covering a total of 311,208 days–or 852 years–before and during the pandemic. To deal with such a large volume of data, the scientists focused their analysis on mammals and how they reacted when human pressure increased again as pandemic restrictions eased. They also directly measured human activity with the camera traps.

In a study published March 18 in *Nature Ecology & Evolution*, Burton and colleagues analyzed these data and found what Burton calls "an incredible amount of variation in what people and animals were doing."

In general, two broad patterns stood out. First, animals' responses depended in large part on their position on the food chain, also known as their trophic level (such as carnivore, omnivore, or herbivore). And second, the degree to which a location has been modified by people played a big role.

Carnivores, the scientists found, were less active when people were around, regardless of location (though large predators such as mountain lions were mostly absent from more developed areas). Among the most sensitive species were wolverines, which became much less active in Alberta's Banff National Park, for example, when people returned after the COVID lockdowns.

Unexpectedly, however, as human activity increased in more developed areas, mammals such as deer were generally more active. "We're scratching our heads," trying to explain this, Burton says. One possible factor would be that humans may act as "shields" against carnivores because the latter might be more skittish and retiring when humans are around–something herbivores such as mule deer seemed to have learned. It also probably has to do with acclimatization; Burton says that increased deer activity in Golden Ears, for example, may be partly caused by the "human shield" phenomenon, whereas in the more remote Pacific Rim park, the herbivores may have been more sensitive and averse to human presence to start with.

This pattern held true for omnivores such as brown and black bears, too—to an extent. These species sometimes became more abundant when human activity increased in various locations that are more developed. But the bears also became more nocturnal. "They can tolerate humans up to a point," Burton says. This may be because a bigger human presence can mean more resources (more garbage or food scraps, for example), but interactions with people are riskier for a large omnivore than they are for a deer or rabbit.

Sarah Raymond, an ecologist at Cardiff University in Wales who wasn't involved with the new study, says she particularly appreciated how this project—one of the largest camera trap studies ever—highlights "the breadth of responses from different groups of species to human activity, both those groups that are most vulnerable, such as carnivores, and those situations where populations appear to actually be attracted to anthropogenic resources or better adapted to living alongside humans."

We need studies like this, she says, because "we're so entrenched in the Anthropocene ecosystem that we overlook the effects that we're having on the environment."

Burton hopes the study results will help humans and animals better co-exist in the world. For example, one potential application of these findings could be to dissuade human nighttime activities in parks and suburban open spaces because many animals, including foxes and bobcats, become more nocturnal in modified landscapes with significant levels of obvious human presence. "In areas where we're sharing space, we need to think about giving [animals] the opportunity to use resources when we're not around," Burton says. "As we push into that nighttime space, we might be affecting those animals."

Ultimately, the study also underscores how some of the "nature is healing" anecdotes that came out during the early days of the pandemic were intriguing—but misleading. "We can't just roll back the clock and keep people out of many areas," Burton says. "We have to be practical about how to find that co-existence balance going forward."

About the Author

Douglas Main is an independent journalist who covers environmental issues, the natural world and a range of other scientific topics. His writing has appeared in the New York Times, the Atlantic, MIT Technology Review, Hakai Magazine *and other publications. Until recently, he was a senior writer and editor at* National Geographic. *Follow him on X (formerly Twitter) at @douglas_main.*

The Pandemic Disrupted Adolescent Brain Development

By Gary Stix

Before COVID, American teenagers' psychological health was already in decline. The pandemic, with its sudden lockdowns, school closures, and other jolts to normal life, made that downward slope steeper. The ensuing mental health crisis has given researchers a rare opportunity to gauge how an extraordinary event such as a public health catastrophe can physically affect the brains of teenagers.

Preliminary results for some of these studies are starting to be reported—and they are sobering. At the annual Society for Neuroscience conference in Washington, D.C., this week, Elizabeth Powell, a program officer at the National Institutes of Health, characterized the situation as a definitive disruption in normal adolescent brain development.

In one set of research results presented at the conference, Patricia Kuhl of the University of Washington reported a larger-than-normal thinning of the cerebral cortex in a group of 124 adolescents who had been tracked before the pandemic at ages nine to 17 and then again after the COVID lockdown period. "Our findings indicate that the teenage brain showed accelerated aging due to the pandemic lockdown," she said at the conference.

Kuhl, a professor and co-director of the Institute of Learning & Brain Sciences at the University of Washington, and her team first took neuroimaging measurements of the participants' brains in 2018. The researchers then compared the amount of brain thinning in 2021 with a computer model of what would usually be expected three years after the point at which the first measurements were made. The cortex normally gets thinner as an adolescent grows, but the model showed a sped-up pattern of thinning during the pandemic. The effect was much more noticeable in female adolescents in the 68 brain areas measured. "The magnitude of this shift in [female adolescents] is quite large," Kuhl said. "A girl who visited the lab, on average, at age 11 and then returned to the lab for time two at age 14 showed the age of a 16-year-old."

Kuhl and her team, who have yet to publish their findings, have more work to do, but the study supports the findings of similar research looking at the impact of the pandemic on brain development. Thinning of the cortex can be a sign of stress. It can affect neuroplasticity, the ability to learn new things; the researchers are still trying to determine whether plasticity was affected in the group study. Kuhl is looking at how cortical thinning may affect language, cognition, and social and emotional well-being, and she and her team are also considering the impact of social media on teens.

Additionally, researchers are examining pandemic health effects from another perspective: How well were adolescent brains prepared to weather such an event? Adolescence is a time when brain circuits typically undergo substantive upheavals. "It is really important to understand the brain as a potential risk or protective factor that could have predisposed youth to mental health issues and/or may have amplified negative emotions and stress during the COVID-19 pandemic," said Caterina Stamoulis, an associate professor at Harvard Medical School, describing unpublished research at the conference. "And it's important to understand that so that we can develop better interventions for these youth."

Stamoulis and her colleagues looked at neuroimaging data from 1,414 adolescents in the Adolescent Brain Cognitive Development Study, the largest ongoing U.S. study of brain development and child health. They examined the organization of brain networks and assessed the strength of connections in neural circuits and how efficiently those circuits processed information.

Less robust circuits in some brain networks foretold greater levels of reported sadness and other stresses among adolescents when these measurements were made in 2020 and 2021 (the two principal years of the pandemic). "We find that the organization of the developing–and vulnerable, therefore–brain circuits may have played a critical role in adolescent mental health, stress, and emotional responses during the COVID-19 pandemic," Stamoulis noted.

About the Author

Gary Stix, senior editor of mind and brain at Scientific American, *edits and reports on emerging advances that have propelled brain science to the forefront of the biological sciences. Stix has edited or written cover stories, feature articles and news on diverse topics, ranging from what happens in the brain when a person is immersed in thought to the impact of brain implant technology that alleviates mood disorders such as depression. Before taking over the neuroscience beat, Stix, as* Scientific American's *special projects editor, oversaw the magazine's annual single-topic special issues, conceiving of and producing issues on Albert Einstein, Charles Darwin, climate change and nanotechnology. One special issue he edited on the topic of time in all of its manifestations won a National Magazine Award. With his wife Miriam Lacob, Stix is co-author of a technology primer called* Who Gives a Gigabyte? A Survival Guide for the Technologically Perplexed.

Telehealth Is Proving to be a Boon to Cancer and Diabetes Care

By Lydia Denworth

Like many people, I was introduced to telehealth during the pandemic. I met with my psychiatrist virtually, settling onto my couch instead of hers for our sessions. But those appointments required only a conversation. It made sense that psychotherapy easily made a switch to the online world.

What's more surprising is how often telehealth now is being used in other medical areas, such as in cancer care. Although chemotherapy and immunotherapy are typically done in person, follow-up visits and medication and symptom management can be done virtually, says Leah Rosengaus, director of digital health at Stanford Health Care in California, where 44 percent of oncology visits are virtual. For patients with cancer receiving routine treatment, that equals a lot less hassle. And for a patient with a poor prognosis, it might be even more meaningful. "The biggest gift [we can] give them is time," Rosengaus says.

Telehealth programs made up less than 1 percent of all health care in the U.S. until March 2020, when, of course, everything changed. The pandemic restricted personal contact, and telehealth surged. (At Stanford, it went from less than 2 percent to more than 70 percent of visits in just a few weeks.) State and federal regulators relaxed rules that required doctors to see patients personally before offering care, and insurers began to cover virtual visits. Now the use of technology such as video chats, secure messaging, and even old-school phone calls to allow clinicians and patients to communicate appears to be here to stay. It has settled at 10 to 30 percent of patient appointments in many large hospital systems.

In general, the quality of telehealth care seems high. Nearly 87 percent of the time, Mayo Clinic researchers reported in *JAMA Network Open* last fall, an initial virtual diagnosis agreed with a later diagnosis made in person. Oncology and psychiatry proved especially accurate; ear, nose and throat and dermatology appointments—which rely more on physical examinations—were somewhat less so. A 2022 study of more than 500,000 patients found equal or better outcomes for telehealth across 13 of 16 primary care measures, such as management of diabetes and following through on flu shot appointments, when compared with in-person visits.

The quality-of-care results seem highest in the specialties that use telehealth most. Endocrinologists, for instance, like it because their patients get lab work done separately and then discuss results with doctors virtually; surgeons are using it to confer with patients before and after procedures.

Patient satisfaction with these visits is good, according to reports from large health-care systems. People say they like the convenience of virtual care—there is no travel, no parking, no child or pet care to arrange. Sanford Health, which serves a widespread rural population from its base in Sioux Falls, S.D., estimates its patients who used virtual care were spared two and a half million miles of driving in 2022.

In some cases, technology is providing clinicians with better insights into those they care for. Jeremy Cauwels, chief physician at Sanford, says an endocrinologist in his organization now carves out several hours a week for video visits with diabetes patients after discovering how much information about diet and habits he could glean from observing them at home.

People vary in how much of their home life they are willing to show, of course. Whereas some patients would never turn a camera on in the living room, others cheerfully display the insides of their medicine cabinets or refrigerators. "We're getting a window into the patient's lived environment that we never had before," Rosengaus says. "That harkens back to the days of doctors and house calls."

Virtual visits do not work for everything and everyone. In the large 2022 telehealth study, in-office patients were more likely to receive and adhere to some medications, such as statins for cardiovascular disease. Starting "a lifelong medication" is a big decision that may be best suited to an in-person discussion, the authors suggest. Another study found that patients who followed up an emergency hospital visit via telehealth rather than in person were more likely to be readmitted to the hospital.

Clearly, medical providers must fine-tune the best use of this technology. The rest of us will keep finding our comfort level (I draw the line at showing my medicine cabinet). The goal, proponents say, is not simply to increase telehealth use but to optimize it and create a good form of hybrid care they call "clicks and mortar."

This is an opinion and analysis article, and the views expressed by the author or authors are not necessarily those of Scientific American.

About the Author

Lydia Denworth is an award-winning science journalist and contributing editor for Scientific American. *She is author of* Friendship *(W. W. Norton, 2020).*

Section 5: Future of Government Policy

The World Desperately Needs a New Pandemic Treaty

By Lawrence O. Gostin & Alexandra Finch

At the height of the COVID pandemic in March of 2021, 25 heads of government and international agencies issued an extraordinary joint call for a "new international treaty for pandemic preparedness and response," to protect the world from future pandemic threats. The treaty was scheduled for adoption at this year's World Health Assembly, the decision-making body for the World Health Organization. Despite a devastating pandemic that resulted in over 20 million excess deaths, negotiations ground to a halt amid bitter political disagreements.

Yet there was a bright spot. On June 1, the final day of the assembly, nations adopted historic reforms of the International Health Regulations, which govern the international spread of infectious diseases, and extended negotiations on the pandemic treaty to May 2025 or earlier. These decisions reinforced the importance of multilateral institutions and international cooperation. Political will seemed to coalesce around a common desire for a healthier and more secure world.

Here's why a pandemic treaty would be a win for people everywhere, in the Global North and South. Think of a pandemic treaty as a grand social bargain to protect future generations from the devastating and inequitable impacts of pandemics. The global social contract has two objectives: the open exchange of scientific information in real time, and the equitable allocation of medical countermeasures. These objectives are not opposed, but essential and interdependent. Each prong would make us all more secure, and the world fairer.

Countries from the Global North have insisted on open and immediate access to scientific data, and for good reason. Surveillance and epidemiological information, transmitted swiftly, can contain outbreaks at their source and trigger early warning for the world to escalate preparedness and response. Pathogen samples and their genomic sequences are also the lifeblood of new diagnostics, vaccines, and therapeutics. When they are shared with national research institutes, laboratories, and pharmaceutical companies, these data can speed the development of lifesaving medical products—a win-win scenario.

Without rapid and transparent scientific exchange, it could take years, not months, to develop a vaccine—potentially costing millions of lives in a pandemic. So, why have many low- and middle-income countries (LMICs) resisted obligations for open scientific sharing? The reason is that pathogen samples and sequence information are their only political leverage to gain a fair share of the fruits of such sharing, access to countermeasures like vaccines. LMICs point to the Nagoya Protocol, a treaty which requires that benefits arising from the utilization of countries' sovereign genetic resources (including pathogens) are equitably shared. The global social contract, therefore, has a second component of equal importance: the equitable distribution of medical countermeasures.

During the COVID-19 pandemic, countermeasures reached LMICs wildly out of step with public health needs. By late 2021, high-income countries had fully vaccinated 75 percent of their populations while fewer than 2 percent in the poorest countries had received a single dose. These inequities resulted from an unevenly distributed manufacturing ecosystem concentrated in wealthy states. High-income governments prepurchased most of the world's supply of vaccines, causing extreme global scarcity. The U.S. and Europe, in particular, bypassed WHO's COVAX initiative, which was designed to accelerate vaccine production and promote equity in vaccine distribution. Finally, powerful pharmaceutical companies strong-armed LMICs, using coercive measures and one-sided procurement contracts, leaving countries without affordable vaccines at the height of the emergency.

In treaty negotiations, high-income countries understood the need for meaningful mechanisms to advance equity but perhaps did not appreciate the level of distrust, even anger, felt by countries from the Global South after four years of pandemic injustice, undergirded by legacies of health inequity, exploitation and resource extraction.

When LMICs are forced to wait for donations from rich governments and pharmaceutical companies, their experience has always been that lifesaving products come too little, too late. This led to the demand that governments and the private sector equitably share not just medical countermeasures but also the means of their production, including research and manufacturing capacity, know-how and technology. That would allow countries and regions to become self-reliant in producing countermeasures. Again, a benefit to all.

Now negotiators have another full year to forge an agreement. With elections looming in the U.S. and much of the world, there is urgency in forging a global treaty. Failure is not an option because it would unravel international cooperation, making us even more vulnerable to another, increasingly likely, pandemic.

The treaty's most contentious, but potentially most transformative, contribution–its "heart"–is pathogen access and benefit sharing. This requires equitable exchange of scientific information and distribution of vaccines between both North and South. All would share science while manufacturers reserve 20 percent of vaccines to distribute based on worldwide public health need, better curbing the spread of disease.

Disadvantaged nations as well as global health advocates have also called for an end-to-end ecosystem that would treat vaccines, tests and therapeutics as global public goods. Smaller pharmaceutical companies will need transfer of technologies and know-how, sustained financing, and flexibility in intellectual property rights, to make these locally.

Up to 75 percent of new and emerging infectious diseases, like SARS, mpox, Ebola, and likely COVID, are caused by spillovers from animals. They cause 2.5 billion global illnesses and 2.7 million deaths each year. A deep prevention, one-health approach, which recognizes human, animal and environmental health interconnections, would limit these spillovers. Industries have opposed these measures, but by the close of the recent treaty negotiations, a path had emerged to their inclusion.

We should make this investment. Many smaller countries still face fiscal constraints limiting any new commitments made under the treaty. They need an additional $10.5 billion per year for preparedness, but have been allocated only $312.7 million from the World Bank's Pandemic Fund, which itself remains badly underfunded. The worldwide COVID-19 mortality cost was $29.4 trillion as of January 2023. Pandemic preparedness is among the most cost-effective measures for high-income countries.

Populist leaders worldwide view international relations as a zero-sum game: "We win, you lose." But the truth is there is mutual benefit in international cooperation, and to a strong pandemic treaty. The biggest threat to global health now is indifference, inaction and a failure to learn the lessons of the COVID pandemic. Let's adopt a pandemic treaty and codify a global social bargain where everyone wins.

This is an opinion and analysis article, and the views expressed by the author or authors are not necessarily those of Scientific American.

Author's Note: Lawrence Gostin is a member of the WHO Review Committee regarding amendments to the International Health Regulations (2005), directs the WHO Collaborating Center on National and Global Health Law and has been actively supporting WHO and the Intergovernmental Negotiating Body on the pandemic treaty.

About the Authors

Lawrence O. Gostin is Distinguished University Professor (Georgetown University's highest academic rank) and Founding O'Neill Chair in Global Health Law and a professor of medicine at Georgetown. He is also director of the World Health Organization Collaborating Center for National and Global Health Law. Follow Gostin on X (formerly Twitter) @lawrencegostin.

Alexandra Finch is an associate at the O'Neill Institute for National and Global Health Law and an adjunct professor of law at Georgetown University Law Center. She previously worked at the United Nations in the Office of the Victims' Rights Advocate.

We Need an Operation Warp Speed for Long COVID

By Esther K. Choo & Scott Duke Kominers

Long COVID is a multifaceted condition that can follow SARS-CoV-2 (COVID-19) infection and affects the neurologic, cardiovascular, pulmonary, hematologic, and endocrine systems, leading to anything from mild to debilitating disease. From a public health perspective, the effects of long COVID are massive; a recent review published in *Nature* estimated that at least 65 million people worldwide have already experienced it.

In August 2022, the Brookings Institution estimated that long COVID is keeping the equivalent of 2 million to 4 million full-time workers out of the American labor force, resulting in about $170 billion of lost earnings per year. Economist David Cutler drew similar conclusions and, moreover, estimated the U.S. health costs of long COVID to be on the order of $100 billion per year. These combined estimates imply a real cost of more than $1 trillion over a five-year period, even before accounting for lost quality of life, increased disability costs, and the burden on caregivers and the health care system. In our roles observing the health and economic toll of long COVID, these accumulating effects are breathtaking and extremely concerning.

And yet, unlike our earliest responses to acute COVID, there is no "Operation Warp Speed" for long COVID.

Because each new COVID infection carries with it the potential to lead to long COVID, the best way to avoid it is to avoid getting infected with COVID in the first place. However, we have largely abandoned societywide measures to prevent disease transmission, making infections difficult to avoid. This means we are forced to fall back on preventing and treating long COVID—but at this point, we can't. Even as caseloads and the suffering of the people who care for those with long COVID continue to mount, science around this aspect of disease lacks transformative investment and activity.

The resources mustered by federal agencies, private companies, and philanthropists to combat long COVID pale in comparison to those dedicated to the development of acute COVID vaccines, tests and treatments. To gain perspective, we searched the NIH's research repository using the terms "Long COVID," "Post-acute sequelae of SARS-CoV-2," "PACS," "Post-COVID syndrome," or "Long haul" (access date March 23, 2023). We found $740.8 million of federal funding for long COVID studies across 218 projects, most of which ($509 million) was allocated in 2021. This reflects only 6% percent of the $11.6 billion in funding and only 2.7 percent of the 8,042 projects dedicated to COVID research overall. Compared to 2021, the percentage of funds devoted to studying long COVID in 2022 was cut by nearly half (from 11 percent to 6 percent)–representing an even bigger drop than it might seem because total COVID research funding decreased over that time period as well.

In March 2020, people began sharing their experiences with illness after acute infection with COVID, leading to the name "long COVID." Yet, it was more than two years later before the Department of Health and Human Services (DHHS) released a "National Research Action Plan on Long COVID." This plan announced an Office of Long COVID Research and Practice which has yet to launch. The RECOVER Initiative, aiming to better understand the long-term effects of the disease, has dedicated just $1.15 billion to long COVID research for the next four years. This amount is disproportionate to the scale of the problem. Moreover, scientists and patient advocates have criticized the distribution of these funds as inefficient and opaque. A report by the Rockefeller Foundation earlier this year noted the NIH had funded only eight of 200 active clinical trials on long COVID registered in clinicaltrials.gov and recommended a broad range of long COVID research improvements, including better data sharing, transparency, coordination, leadership, patient engagement, and information dissemination.

"The world knows too little about long COVID, and this must change," the Rockefeller report stated, calling upon the NIH to accelerate its ongoing long COVID research. The private sector response has been even more dismal. Biotech and pharma have largely "skirted" the issue of long COVID, entering the effort in a substantial way only in mid-2022.

No doubt, long COVID's myriad symptoms present a challenge for developing therapeutics. Perhaps the potential return on investment is less clear for long COVID than with vaccines and treatments. But the continued narrative that COVID is no worse than a cold when it does not lead to hospitalizations and deaths utterly dismisses the significance of long COVID, which can occur even after mild infections. As a nation, we cannot accelerate and amply fund science around long COVID while failing to take it seriously.

The world's extraordinary progress on COVID vaccines and therapeutics has shown what a coordinated effort across government and industry can accomplish in short order for the public good. A "Warp Speed" response to long COVID could lead to a better understanding of long COVID's risk factors, whether and how much vaccines and acute treatments protect against long COVID and how such protection may vary depending on factors such as vaccine type and number, therapeutic treatment, COVID variant and viral load. We need to know much more about how to define, diagnose and classify long COVID to enable health-care professionals to recognize it more consistently and provide the nation with a more accurate understanding of its incidence and prevalence. And health care providers and those living with long COVID urgently need more guidance to inform support, prognosis, and care.

With momentum, political will, and multisector funding, we could explore multiple potential pathways of disease at once, including autonomic nervous system damage, immune scarring, viral persistence and coagulation activation. And while further basic research may be required to fully understand some pathways, we do not need to wait on those results to begin to develop treatments for the chronic inflammation and coagulation disorders that we already know afflict long COVID sufferers.

We all wish the pandemic were behind us. But with an ever-growing number of people wrestling with a baffling disease, too little scientific understanding of its mechanism and management, and little effort to avoid its occurrence, we are sustaining the conditions for a long COVID crisis. The reality is that our failure to address long COVID guarantees the pandemic will continue, with dire implications for all of society.

This is an opinion and analysis article, and the views expressed by the author or authors are not necessarily those of Scientific American.

About the Authors

Esther K. Choo is an emergency physician and professor in the Center for Policy and Research in Emergency Medicine in the Department of Emergency Medicine at Oregon Health & Science University. She holds an M.D. from Yale University and an M.P.H. from Oregon Health & Science University.

Scott Duke Kominers is a professor of business administration in the Entrepreneurial Management Unit at Harvard Business School; faculty affiliate in the Harvard Department of Economics and the Harvard Center of Mathematical Sciences and Applications and a research partner at a16z crypto. He holds a Ph.D. from Harvard University.

Bad COVID Public Health Messaging Is Blocking Our Path to a 'New Normal'

By Thoai D. Ngo

The U.S. has no clear vision of how to reach a postpandemic world. Over the past two years, we have developed extraordinary scientific tools for the mitigation, treatment, and prevention of COVID. But we've stumbled badly in implementing them. Many of these failures happened because our public health messages were not clear about how to use those tools, which include vaccines, masks, tests, antiviral drugs, and temporary activity restrictions. The result is confusion among the public that has left us vulnerable to the disease and unable to respond to new and more transmissible variants such as BA.2 and its sublineages, which are infecting a rising number of people across the nation. America has already lost 1 million people during this pandemic. There may be future mutations that could be more lethal and highly contagious, and we are still woefully unprepared for them.

Recovering from these mistakes will require a bold change in direction for our national health messages. Now, as cases rise, it is an opportune time for the Biden administration to launch a new communications campaign through the Centers for Disease Control and Prevention (CDC), one with the resources and structure to prepare Americans to move forward. The campaign must begin by drawing a line in the sand: how many deaths are we willing to tolerate? Can we accept 50,000 deaths per year as part of our "new normal"? 100,000? With our hard-won ability to prevent deaths from the disease, it would be morally abhorrent to lose tens of thousands more Americans to COVID. These deaths orphan hundreds of thousands of children and, along with the serious illnesses, destroy an entire generation of older Americans, rip apart family structure, and wreak havoc on the economy.

At the start of the year, the Omicron variant made our vulnerability painfully clear. A surge of cases caused by this highly transmissible version of the virus completely disrupted American society, causing 3.6 million work absences in January alone. Hospitals, already struggling with staff shortages, burnout and inadequate resources, were once again overloaded. Failures in containment made the relatively mild variant far deadlier than the dangerous Delta variant that preceded it. In February, the country was averaging more than 15,000 COVID deaths per week. The million deaths we have suffered is a record far worse than any other wealthy nation.

Why have we failed to protect ourselves? A major reason is that federal agencies focused on a vaccination-only strategy when inoculations became available. Their erratic efforts to pursue other safety measures have been infrequent, and slow, and have often been rejected by the courts. On the local level, governments have rushed to abandon almost all mitigation strategies, from mask mandates to vaccination requirements. The manners in which measures have been introduced and rescinded vary widely across state and county lines, which has caused confusion about how dangerous the virus continues to be and what precautions remain necessary.

The COVID-19 Community Levels assessment issued by the CDC is an example of a whiplash change in messaging that confuses more people than it helps. At the end of February, the CDC switched overnight from a tool focused on new infections to one that relies primarily on hospital admissions and occupancy. As a result, many counties that were previously high-risk zones suddenly became low-risk. The agency added new recommendations for behavior to these altered ratings. For instance, it no longer recommends masking indoors for medium-risk counties. The change seems hard to justify: there is a delay of three to 10 days between symptom onset and hospitalization, one 2020 study reported, and this causes a consistent lag between spikes in reported cases and the consequent increase in hospitalizations. With new cases poorly tracked and their trends deemphasized, the new system will be much less useful for everyday decision-making about getting on a bus or train or going into a crowded office.

Worse, many of these CDC recommendations leave decisions completely up to personal and idiosyncratic judgements. Visit any gym in the country and you'll find members taking care to disinfect treadmills and weights, even while exercising without a mask in poorly ventilated spaces. These poorly protective behaviors reflect CDC messaging. Agency messages place vaccination and masking at the top of their list of preventive measure lists, but do little to differentiate the importance of these measures from those that matter far less, such as cleaning surfaces. The CDC still does not clearly recommend the use of N95 and KN95 masks, even though robust evidence for the superior effectiveness of N95s was available for years before the pandemic began. Instead the agency equivocates, emphasizing comfort and stating people should "wear the most protective mask you can that fits well and that you will wear consistently." In January of this year, the agency finally clarified that N95-type masks types are more protective than others. (Early in the pandemic it had warned Americans away from these masks because of concerns about supply shortages for medical workers).

In some cases, changes of CDC positions were prompted by shifts in our scientific understanding of the disease. But in many others, the changes appear to be arbitrary or to be driven by public pressure and business interests. In December 2021, the agency reduced recommended isolation periods for infected health care workers from 10 days down to seven, adding that "isolation time can be cut further if there are staffing shortages." A week later, they shortened recommended isolation and quarantine periods for the general population down to just five days, irrespective of whether a person was still infectious, and did not require a negative test result. Yet the agency itself notes that "people can continue to spread the virus another [eight] days after their symptoms began."

The CDC's director, Rochelle Walensky, acknowledged that the goal was to allow people to "continue their daily lives." Several experts noted, however, that while the move was necessary to prevent economic strain in certain sectors, a five-day isolation period, and no test requirement were not sufficient to minimize risk.

This year Walensky gave the public mixed messages on mask wearing. In an interview on February 21 she described donning a mask as "easy" and "painless" but also called the protective coverings "the scarlet letter" of the pandemic. She added that they were "annoying" and a barrier to "living our lives normally." These contradictory statements about a critical lifesaving tool added a dangerous stigma to it, and are a real failure in public health communications.

A new and successful communications campaign has to start by defining how much death and disease, going forward, the country can accept from this virus. The administration must bring together public health experts to set these targets at low, achievable numbers. Then Congress—which has recently balked at spending money on prevention and treatment—must commit resources to match them.

It is also urgent for the federal government to publicize useful yardsticks for when and how people should use masks, social distancing, and mass testing. These tools are highly effective but difficult to continue for long periods, so everyone needs to understand when they need to be implemented and when they can be stopped. Those short-term measures should be framed as protections and should be easy for the public to adopt when key metrics begin to rise. They must be accompanied by multiple fallback plans that are also widely publicized, so that the public is ready to respond as the pandemic continues to shift and evolve.

Reaching and motivating the public will also require substantial long-term changes to how we disseminate public health information. These efforts need to go far beyond CDC guidelines and academic articles; we need celebrity involvement, interactive (and appealing) online media, educational materials and broadcasts, and in-person outreach. We need ambassadors and voices from different communities, particularly those that are more marginalized or more at risk, and materials in multiple languages.

The reality is that local governments and courts have made this kind of coordination difficult through active resistance to federal guidance. But their opposition was enabled by the absence of a clear top-down vision beginning with the Trump administration, frequent vacillation on key pieces of guidance, and the repeated failure to establish links between guidance and underlying science. Consistent and sustained public messaging can also serve as a countermeasure against misinformation and disinformation.

We know far more about how to treat COVID and mitigate the risks than we did two years ago. But we have failed to translate this knowledge into clear messaging capable of prompting collective action to move us toward a "new normal." A nationwide public health communication strategy that is consistent and as free as possible from political influence is urgently needed to close the space between knowledge and action.

This is an opinion and analysis article, and the views expressed by the author or authors are not necessarily those of Scientific American.

About the Author

Thoai D. Ngo is the vice president of social and behavioral science research at the Population Council. An epidemiologist based in New York City, he focuses his research on the intersections between gender, health and poverty globally. He holds a Ph.D. from the London School for Hygiene and Tropical Medicine. Follow Ngo on X (formerly Twitter) @ThoaiDNgo.

Universal Health Care Could Have Saved More Than 330,000 U.S. Lives during COVID

By Rachel Nuwer

Americans spend more on health care than people in any other nation. Yet in any given year, the piecemeal nature of the American medical insurance system causes many preventable deaths and unnecessary costs. Not surprisingly, COVID only exacerbated this already dire public health issue, as evidenced by the U.S.'s elevated mortality, compared with that of other high-income countries.

A recent study quantified the severity of the impact of the pandemic on Americans who did not have access to health insurance. According to findings published in June 2022 in the *Proceedings of the National Academy of Sciences USA*, from the pandemic's beginning until mid-March 2022, universal health care could have saved more than 338,000 lives from COVID alone. The U.S. also could have saved \$105.6 billion in health-care costs associated with hospitalizations from the disease—on top of the estimated \$438 billion that could be saved in a nonpandemic year.

"Health-care reform is long overdue in the U.S.," says the study's lead author Alison Galvani, director of the Center for Infectious Disease Modeling and Analysis at the Yale School of Public Health. "Americans are needlessly losing lives and money."

People who do not have insurance usually do not have a primary care doctor, which means they are more likely to suffer from preventable diseases such as type 2 diabetes. They also tend to wait longer to see a doctor when they fall ill. These two factors already contribute to higher mortality rates in nonpandemic years, and they compounded the impacts of COVID. Comorbidities exacerbate the risk of the disease, and waiting to seek care increases the likelihood of transmission to other people.

Prior to the pandemic, 28 million American adults were uninsured, and 9 million more lost their insurance as a result of unemployment because of COVID. "Many Americans feel secure in having good health insurance from their employer, but employer-based insurance can be cut off when it is needed most," Galvani points out.

In the study, Galvani's team compared the mortality risks of COVID among people with and without insurance, as well as their risks of all other causes of death. The researchers compiled population characteristics of all uninsured Americans during the pandemic, taking into account things such as age-specific life expectancy and the elevation in mortality associated with a lack of insurance. They calculated that 131,438 people could have been saved from dying of COVID in 2020 alone. And more than 200,000 additional deaths from COVID could have been averted between then and the end of the study, bringing the total through March 12, 2022, to more than 338,000.

The researchers also estimated the cost to insure the entire U.S. population–and the savings that measure would produce. They found that a single-payer health-care system would generate savings in three ways: more efficient investment in preventive care; lowered administrative costs; and increased negotiating power for pharmaceuticals, equipment, and fees. This would have produced a net savings of $459 billion in 2020 and $438 billion in a nonpandemic year, the authors found. "Medicare for All would be both an economic stimulus and lifesaving transformation of our health-care system," Galvani says. "It will cost people far less than the status quo."

Galvani and her colleagues' findings are "very convincing," and "the methodology strikes me as exactly right," says Robert Reich, a professor of public policy at the University of California, Berkeley, who was not involved in the work. "The savings estimates are consistent with every other estimate I've seen."

Ann Keller, an associate professor of health policy and management also at U.C. Berkeley, suspects, however, that the study likely underestimates the deaths that could have been avoided through universal health care because it does not consider the lower rates of chronic disease that often accompany single-payer systems. "Having consistent access to care can prevent chronic disease from occurring and can ensure that patients who develop chronic disease have it better managed," says Keller, who was also not involved with the research. "I would think that, if one took that into account, the estimates of avoided deaths would be greater than the numbers reported here."

Whatever the exact figures, Galvani says the message that comes out of the study is clear: "Universal single-payer health care is both economically responsible and morally imperative."

About the Author

Rachel Nuwer is a science journalist and author. Her latest book is I Feel Love: MDMA and the Quest for Connection in a Fractured World *(Bloomsbury, 2023). Follow her on X @RachelNuwer.*

Contagions Worse Than COVID Will Prevail if Neglect of Global Public Health Continues

By The Editors

After Omicron comes *pi* in the Greek alphabet. And then *rho, sigma, tau*.... Before SARS-CoV-2 finishes its grand tour through the Greek alphabet, the global public health establishment should do what it should have done long before this coronavirus emerged. It must put in place the basic health systems needed to detect new outbreaks and deploy technologies that allow for vaccines and medicines to be manufactured and administered in low- and middle-income countries.

Because they have often refused to treat COVID as a common threat that demands a unified response, policy makers have yet to thwart the predations of a virus that, to channel the Greeks again, affects all (*pan*) people (*demos*). This myopia means that these mistakes could be repeated when a new pandemic arrives.

The next time could be worse. The National Academy of Medicine predicted in November 2021 that a flu epidemic akin to the one in 1918 and 1919 could prove more catastrophic than COVID-19. The preconditions for such a disaster are in place. A warming planet, megacities, mass migration, intercontinental travel, and habitat loss are among the reasons that infectious diseases, like intensifying typhoons and hurricanes, have become part of our lives.

Fast-tracked development of diagnostics, vaccines, monoclonal antibodies, and antiviral drugs marks an undisputed medical triumph of the COVID era. Also notable, however, is the failure of governments and international organizations to use our current predicament to rectify glaring public health deficiencies.

The Global Health Security Index for 2021 rated the world's 195 countries as "dangerously unprepared" to deal with future epidemic and pandemic threats. The average score for individual countries came in at 38.9 out of 100, about the same as the 2019 rating—before the pandemic began. Many countries failed to grasp that the pandemic presented an unparalleled opportunity to lay the groundwork for coping with not only this public health crisis but also future ones.

Readiness for a COVID-30 or a new pandemic flu strain—or, for that matter, an out-of-control bioweapon—will require new generations of surveillance tools, diagnostics, and drugs, as well as, say, a "universal" coronavirus vaccine that can counter any strain. Having sufficient available vaccine formulations with long shelf lives would also help alleviate the inequities that have accompanied distribution of shots. Underscoring the absence of "global" in "global public health," Portugal had fully vaccinated 89 percent of its population by mid-January 2022 but Mali only 2.8 percent.

The most pressing priority should be a return to basics, both globally and locally. COVID has served as a painful demonstration that public health is as essential to national security as a standing army. And the cost of health security is minimal. In 2016 the Commission on a Global Health Risk Framework for the Future estimated that for 65 cents a year for every person on the planet, we could upgrade national pandemic preparedness programs worldwide. An investment of $4.5 billion—far less than the price of a single new ballistic missile submarine—might prevent the global loss of millions of lives and an economic hit in the trillions of dollars.

The basics entail not only building new systems to prepare for pandemics but a major strengthening of institutions already in place. Public health legal expert Lawrence O. Gostin has noted that the World Health Organization had a 2022–2023 budget of $6.12 billion, which is less than those of some major U.S. teaching hospitals. The WHO needs not just money but reforms that give it the authority to better monitor and intervene when new infectious diseases emerge. At the country level, the most basic of basics consists of functioning national systems that furnish medical care for all and financial help, as needed, for child care, food, housing, and other measures to waylay the poverty-related chronic diseases capable of sending even a relatively young adult onto a ventilator during a future pandemic.

After repeated outbreaks of horrific diseases such as SARS, Ebola, and Zika, perhaps this calamity will prove traumatic enough to bring about a coherent remake of the current system. Deaths from COVID worldwide by late October 2022 nearly equaled the population of Lebanon—and the pandemic is still with us. Only when global public health commands the attention of policy makers in the same way as a new contract for nuclear submarines will Greek letters return to their more familiar role in American life as naming conventions for student groups on college campuses.

COVID Revealed the Fragility of American Public Health

By Wendy E. Parmet

Epidemics expose a society's vulnerabilities. And we were already an unhealthy population before COVID emerged. Compared with some other developed countries, the U.S. has extraordinary rates of chronic obstructive pulmonary disease, diabetes, and other afflictions that leave people more susceptible to severe COVID. These vulnerabilities were influenced strongly by social factors–not purely genetics.

How did we get here? Partially it was because our public health system had been depleted and eroded. Public health has long been the second-class cousin of the individual health-care system, even though they are closely related. In recent history, we spent lots of money on individual treatment and invested far less in *population* health. Public health systems lacked adequate personnel, data systems for analysis, the latest technology, and government support.

Adding to an already perilous situation, the pandemic exposed and accelerated preexisting trends in our society, such as growing distrust of institutions, including of science. In the past 20 years or more, American conservatism transformed to antiscience populism. Even in the legal sphere, there has been a dramatic change in the past year in how many courts, including the U.S. Supreme Court, look at public health–a shift from perhaps being excessively deferential to public health policies to becoming hostile to public health, embracing an antiregulatory approach that spans various doctrinal categories.

With such a great push toward individualism, populism, and a judicial review that is skeptical of public health, how do we keep the gains we've made against childhood diseases such as polio and measles, chronic illnesses such as those caused by smoking, and motor vehicle accidents? Life expectancy climbed in the 20th century not only because of tremendous scientific advancements and increasing wealth but also because public health campaigns and public health laws accomplished a lot. In the backlash against COVID restrictions and policy, we risk undoing all that.

About the Author

Wendy E. Parmet is faculty co-director of Northeastern University's Center for Health Policy and Law.

COVID Models Show How to Avoid Future Lockdowns

By Stacey McKenna

As cases of COVID-19 surge to record levels across the United States, national public health advisors Anthony Fauci and Deborah Birx have pushed for an approach that emphasizes intensive social distancing and widespread mask use, and many states are striving to slow the virus's spread without resorting to complete lockdowns. That strategy helped some states mitigate their outbreaks through the summer. But with winter and major holidays coming, will such measures be enough?

Scientists have already begun incorporating various degrees of social distancing and mask use into their predictions of the pandemic's course. The models have gotten more sophisticated and responsive during the course of the pandemic. They all show with high degrees of certainty that masking and distancing save lives. And increasingly, they put a number on how these behaviors determine how many people will live or die.

To predict COVID transmission during the holidays, Colorado simulates several scenarios. The most important variable is called "transmission control," which is defined as "the percent decrease in effective contacts between infected and susceptible individuals compared to pre-pandemic behavior." This measure accounts for a wide range of behavioral and policy changes, which include wearing masks, physical distancing, moving activities outdoors, and contact tracing. On November 4, based on the state's then trajectory with 62 percent transmission control, the model projected that 8,500 Colorado residents will have died of COVID by the end of the year; on November 20, with 65 percent transmission control, the model reduced that projection to 6,560. But if social contacts increase and interactions were more risky before and through the holiday season, the model had earlier estimated as many as

17,500 virus-related deaths in the state by December 31. If, however, Colorado residents improve transmission control in the coming weeks to reach 80 percent (a level achieved over the summer), cumulative fatalities are projected at 5,500.

Such predictions trend nationally, as well. In a recent paper in *Nature Medicine*, a forecasting team from the University of Washington's Institute for Health Metrics and Evaluation (IHME) ran five scenarios based on social distancing mandates and masking. Their findings suggest that universal mask use (defined as 95 percent of people wearing face coverings in public), combined with states shutting down if they exceed eight deaths per day per million people, "could be sufficient to ameliorate the worst effects of epidemic resurgences in many states." Compared with a scenario in which 49 percent of people wear masks in public, and shutdowns resume at the above threshold for deaths, the authors estimated that universal masking could save nearly 130,000 lives between September 22, 2020 and the end of February 2021.

Dealing with Uncertainty

For months, health-care systems and state and local policy makers have been working with modelers to help anticipate hospital needs; the IHME models were originally developed for this purpose. But looking to models for absolute answers comes with its own set of challenges. Early in the pandemic, as public health experts urged citizens to take the novel coronavirus seriously, they cited predictions estimating that the U.S. would see anywhere from tens of thousands to more than 2 million deaths. The wide ranges between various models, as well as discrepancies between predictions and actual deaths, led experts to criticize the models and made the public wary of the modeling process itself. Indeed, scientists challenged the latest IHME model for seeking to make predictions so far into the future. IHME program director Christopher Murray said in an October press briefing that even though the model's median error is approximately 20 percent for long-range forecasts, this is still better than most other public models. "Clearly uncertainty grows as you go into the future," Murray noted. But "the key point here is that there's a huge winter surge coming, and our models have been showing that for many months."

Any one model may prove more or less appropriate for a particular purpose. But a degree of uncertainty is always expected, explains Rebecca Morrison, an assistant professor of computer science at University of Colorado Boulder. She has previously modeled chemical reactions, as well as ecological and epidemiological scenarios. By definition, she says, models seek to simplify the world; otherwise they would not be useful to us. Epidemiologists who use them must make choices and depend on assumptions about a variety of factors such as individual behavior, how the disease spreads or what percent of the population is immune.

Ideally these assumptions reflect the constantly shifting reality on the ground, says Ali Mokdad, a professor of health metrics sciences at IHME and chief strategy officer for population health at the University of Washington. For example, he says, the IHME team based one assumption–that social distancing mandates would be reimposed for six weeks in communities where daily deaths reached eight people per million–on when most governments actually imposed lockdowns. But because human behavior changes (and because our knowledge remains limited about COVID-19 and SARS-CoV-2, the virus that causes it), Mokdad says models must be dynamic. "If your model is assuming that a relationship is going to hold true throughout the [entire time] period, that's the problem," he says. "We keep updating our model, including new data as it comes to us, and then we reevaluate every time what we see and what's the relationship."

This kind of agility may be key to Vermont's widely lauded pandemic response. Michael Pieciak, who is the state's commissioner of financial regulation and has taken the lead on analytics and modeling of the pandemic there, credits much of this success to a willingness to use state data and work flexibly with internal and external experts. Vermont has not only committed to making data-driven decisions, he says, but also to examining and evaluating its models on a regular basis. "You want to get as honest a view of [the data] as possible, and continue to refine [the model] to move forward," Pieciak says.

Despite all this uncertainty, a recent analysis of 131 countries suggests that moderately severe restrictions–applied individually and in combination–have slowed transmission of SARS-CoV-2 to varying degrees. The researchers found, for example, that banning public events and gatherings of more than 10 people could reduce the reproduction number *R* (the estimated number of people being infected by one infectious individual) by as much as 29 percent a month after implementation. Add workplace closures to the mix, and *R* would decrease by approximately 38 percent. However, says the paper's senior author Harish Nair, a professor of global health at the University of Edinburgh, choosing which interventions to implement "would depend on where in the trajectory of the epidemic [a locale is]. For example, if your *R* is 1.5, you can use a combination of less severe measures–whereas if it [is] over 2, you would need to go into a lockdown." That is because so long as *R* stays above 1, cases will continue to increase.

With community transmission now widespread throughout the country and *R* above 1 in the vast majority of states, prevention is likely off the table. But governments that embrace the science on distancing and mask use might be able to blunt the impact. As state and local authorities try to avoid both lockdowns and hospital overloads, many are in fact using specifics gleaned from contact tracing–such as a plurality of cases deriving from small private gatherings–to guide new restrictions. "We are coming into a very hard and difficult time," Mokdad says. "We really need to be ready, and we need to do our part."

About the Author

Stacey McKenna is a medical anthropologist and freelance journalist who writes about science, travel, and all things equine.

GLOSSARY

acute In a disease, one that has a rapid onset and lasts a relatively short amount of time.

biohazard A biological substance that is hazardous to humans, animals, and/or the environment.

cognitive Having to do with intellectual activity and reasoning.

diagnostic The practice of testing to determine a medical diagnosis.

endemic Having to do with a disease that's restricted to a particular area.

enzyme A protein made by living cells that causes biochemical processes.

epidemiologist A type of scientist who deals with the cause and location of diseases.

genome The genetic material of an organism.

interferon A protein released by cells to try to stop a virus from replicating.

malady A disease or disorder.

neurological Having to do with the nervous system.

pathogen A bacterium or virus that can cause a disease.

pharmacological Having to do with therapeutic drugs.

phylogenetic Relating to the evolution of an organism.

pulmonary Having to do with the lungs.

regimen A systemic plan.

replicate To duplicate.

spectrometry Using instruments to measure light and wavelengths.

synthetic Something that is created by chemical or biochemical processes.

variant Something that deviates from an original or standard form.

FURTHER INFORMATION

Kreier, Kreda. "Combined COVID-Flu Vaccines Are Coming: Moderna Jab Clears Major Test." *Nature*, June 28, 2024, https://www.nature.com/articles/d41586-024-02121-1.

Kudiabor, Helena. "Long COVID Lung Damage Linked to Immune System Response." *Nature*, July 18, 2024, https://www.nature.com/articles/d41586-024-02352-2.

Lenharo, Mariana. "Global Plan for Dealing with Next Pandemic Just Got Weaker, Critics Say." *Nature*, June 1, 2023, https://www.nature.com/articles/d41586-023-01805-4.

Lewis, Tanya. "COVID's Six-Foot Rule Made Scientific Sense at the Time." *Scientific American*, June 4, 2024, https://www.scientificamerican.com/article/marjorie-taylor-greenes-attacks-of-fauci-over-covids-six-foot-rule-not-based/.

Lewis, Tanya, and Josh Fischman. "Should You Swab Your Throat Plus Your Nose for COVID?" *Scientific American*, March 4, 2024, https://www.scientificamerican.com/podcast/episode/should-you-swab-your-throat-plus-your-nose-for-covid/.

Makin, Simon. "Here's Why Infants Are Strangely Resistant to COVID." *Scientific American*, February 12, 2024, https://www.scientificamerican.com/article/heres-why-infants-are-strangely-resistant-to-covid/.

Mallapaty, Smriti. "The Pathogens That Could Spark the Next Pandemic." *Nature*, August 2, 2024, https://www.nature.com/articles/d41586-024-02513-3.

McCorkell, Lisa, and Michael J. Peluso. "Long COVID Research Risks Losing Momentum—We Need a Moonshot." *Nature*, October 18, 2023, https://www.nature.com/articles/d41586-023-03225-w.

CITATIONS

1.1 Longest-Ever COVID Infection Lasted More Than 600 Days by Riis Williams (May 1, 2024); 1.2 Vaccination Dramatically Lowers Long COVID Risk by Shannon Hall (January 3, 2024); 1.3 The 'Brain Fog' of Long COVID Is a Serious Medical Issue That Needs More Attention by Emily Mendenhall & Kenton Kaplan (May 12, 2023); 1.4 Blood Clotting Proteins Might Help Predict Long COVID Brain Fog by Sara Reardon (September 1, 2023); 1.5 A Tsunami of Disability Is Coming as a Result of 'Long COVID' by Claire Pomeroy (July 6, 2021); 1.6 Long COVID Rates Appear to Be Decreasing by Shannon Hall (December 1, 2023); 1.7 What Tony Fauci Says about Long COVID and Other Postviral Illnesses by Emily Mendenhall (November 10, 2023); 2.1 How Risky Are Repeat COVID Infections? What We Know So Far by Meghan Bartels (February 13, 2024); 2.2 Do Repeat COVID Infections Increase the Risk of Severe Disease or Long COVID? by Charles Schmidt (February 15, 2023); 2.3 Why Some People Haven't Caught COVID despite Being Exposed by Saima S. Iqbal (July 3, 2024); 2.4 What Is Paxlovid Rebound, and How Common Is It? by Fionna M. D. Samuels (August 8, 2022); 2.5 Why Some People Get Sick More Often by Elana Spivack (June 21, 2023); 3.1 A High-Speed Scientific Hive Mind Emerged from the COVID Pandemic by Joseph Bak-Coleman & Carl T. Bergstrom (March 1, 2022); 3.2 5 Things We've Learned from COVID in Three Years by Stephanie Pappas (March 13, 2023); 3.3 Scientists behind mRNA COVID Vaccines Win 2023 Nobel Prize in Physiology or Medicine by Lauren J. Young (October 2, 2023); 3.4 How COVID Changed Science by William A. Haseltine (May 25, 2021); 3.5 Astronomy Tool Can Now Detect COVID in Breath by Starre Vartan (May 12, 2023); 3.6 Zapping the Vagus Nerve Could Relieve Some Long COVID Symptoms by Shi En Kim (December 28, 2023); 3.7 The Pandemic Set Off a Boom in Diagnostics by Roxanne Khamsi (March 1, 2022); 3.8 Pathogen-Sensing Mask Could Detect COVID Infection by Simon Makin (October 1, 2021); 3.9 An Experimental Treatment Could Help COVID Smell Distortion by Hannah Docter-Loeb (December 15, 2023); 4.1 COVID Changed the World of Work Forever by Christina Maslach & Michael P. Leiter (March 1, 2022); 4.2 The Pandemic Showed the Promise of Cities with Fewer Cars by Andrea Thompson (March 1, 2022); 4.3 We Indulged Our Child During COVID Lockdown. Did That Change Him? by Michael Venutolo-Mantovani (July 9, 2024); 4.5 Global Emissions Rebound to Pre-COVID Levels by Rob Jackson, Pierre Friedlingstein, Corinne Le Quéré, Robbie Andrew, Pep Canadell, Glen Peters, & Sam Abernathy (November 11, 2021); 4.6 How Wild Animals Actually Responded to Our COVID Lockdowns by Douglas Main (March 18, 2024); 4.7 The Pandemic Disrupted Adolescent Brain Development by Gary Stix (November 17, 2023); 4.8 Telehealth Is Proving to be a Boon to Cancer and Diabetes Care by Lydia Denworth (April 1, 2023); 5.1 The World Desperately Needs a New Pandemic Treaty by Lawrence O. Gostin & Alexandra Finch (June 19, 2024); 5.2 We Need an Operation Warp Speed for Long COVID by Esther K. Choo & Scott Duke Kominers (April 5, 2023); 5.3 Bad COVID Public Health Messaging Is Blocking Our Path to a 'New Normal' by Thoai D. Ngo (June 15, 2022); 5.4 Universal Health Care Could Have Saved More Than 330,000 U.S. Lives during COVID by Rachel Nuwer (June 13, 2022); 5.5 Contagions Worse Than COVID Will Prevail if Neglect of Global Public Health Continues by The Editors (March 1, 2022); 5.6 COVID Revealed the Fragility of American Public Health by Wendy E. Parmet (March 1, 2022); 5.7 COVID Models Show How to Avoid Future Lockdowns by Stacey McKenna (November 24, 2020).

Each author biography was accurate at the time the article was originally published.

INDEX

W

Z